ACCIDENTS

In North American Climbing 2024

VOLUME 13 | NUMBER 2 | ISSUE 77

AMERICAN ALPINE CLUB
GOLDEN, COLORADO

ALPINE CLUB OF CANADA
CANMORE, ALBERTA

CONTENTS

INTRODUCTION

FEATURE ARTICLES

ACCIDENTS & ANALYSIS

DATA TABLES

Front Cover: Adam Fabrikant high on Denali during a trouble-free ascent of the Cassin Ridge. Photo by Michael Gardner.

Back Cover: Rescue training in Utah's Big Cottonwood Canyon. Helicopters can provide expedited response times and fast access to remote technical terrain. Photo by Dave Weber.

ISBN: 979-8-9874576-6-5. Printed in South Korea. Published by the American Alpine Club, 710 Tenth Street, Suite 100, Golden, CO 80401.

WARNING!
The activities described within Accidents in North American Climbing (ANAC)—including but not limited to: rock climbing, ice climbing, mountaineering, backcountry skiing, or any other outdoor activity—carry a significant risk of personal injury or death. The owners, staff, contributors, and volunteers that create this publication recommend that you DO NOT participate in these activities unless you are an expert, have sought or obtained qualified professional instruction or guidance, are knowledgeable about the risks involved, and are willing to assume personal responsibility for all the risks associated with these activities. ANAC and its publisher, the American Alpine Club, MAKE NO WARRANTIES, EXPRESSED OR IMPLIED, OF ANY KIND REGARDING THE CONTENTS OF THIS PUBLICATION, AND EXPRESSLY DISCLAIM ANY WARRANTY REGARDING THE ACCURACY OR RELIABILITY OF INFORMATION CONTAINED HEREIN. The American Alpine Club further disclaims any responsibility for injuries or death incurred by any person engaging in these activities. Use the information contained in this publication at your own risk, and do not depend on the information contained herein for personal safety or for determining whether to attempt any climb, route, or activity described herein. The examples/stories contained herein are anecdotal and/or informational only and are not intended to represent advice, recommendations, or commentary on appropriate conduct, standards or choices that you, the reader, may make regarding your own activities.

United WE Climb.

As an AAC member, you are linked to a Club of passionate climbers focused on connecting with each other, protecting climbing landscapes, and equipping ourselves with expert climbing knowledge and inspiring stories from the cutting edge.

Leverage your membership—and feed your passion for climbing—by applying to our adventure grants, snagging those discounts, reading up on your Rescue and Medical Expense Benefit, and finding events to connect with your community.

Not a member and feel like you're missing out? Learn more about the Club and join or renew at americanalpineclub.org.

American Alpine Club

ACCIDENTS IN NORTH AMERICAN CLIMBING

VOLUME 13 | NUMBER 2 | ISSUE 77

American Alpine Club

EDITOR EMERITUS
John E. (Jed) Williamson

EDITOR
Pete Takeda

DESIGN
Foster Denney

SENIOR EDITOR
Dave Weber

CONTRIBUTING EDITORS
Aram Attarian (NC) and Lindsay Auble (KY and TN)

REGIONAL EDITORS
Daniel Apodaca (NM and AZ); Mark Berenblum
(NY); Mijanou Colbert (Quebec, CAN); Dan
Cousins (New England); Stefani Dawn (NV); Ian
Jackson (Banff, Yoho, Kootenay, CAN); Ashton
Johnston (CO); Michelle Leber and Sarah Wolfe
(UT); Jesse McGahey (Yosemite); Christine Oken
(Denali); Christy Rosa (CA); Mathew Trotter
(Jasper, CAN); Michael Wejchert (NH)

ADDITIONAL THANKS
Caleb Bryce, Michael Buchanan, Elizabeth
Cromwell, Karsten Delap, Dallas Glass, Dr. Peter
Hackett, Dr. TJ Hartridge, Leo Paik, Scott Turpin

AAC EXECUTIVE EDITOR
Dougald MacDonald

Alpine Club of Canada

CANADA EDITOR
Robert Chisnall

PREFACE

By Pete Takeda

To a large extent, climbing has taught me everything. The act of climbing, its requisite engagement with the natural world, its physical complexities, its emotional breadth, its spiritual depths, its human interactions. For me, nothing else is as complete. Climbing has also taught me to be more human—that is, fallible in both capability and assumption. Climbing accidents have taught me that what I imagine to be true can be faulty or inadequate.

Last year, in one of the many incidents reported in this edition, a very experienced leader, after climbing into a quandary, deliberately hopped off a route in West Virginia while on lead. His rope was cut clean through. His rope was not running over an edge, his gear was in perfect working order, and his partner made no mistakes.

Last year, several climbers reported that they fell either deliberately or incidentally on bolted sport routes, and in the process their carabiners broke. In each case, there was no fault in the hardware, nor was there any notable user error.

Last year, a climber fell, unroped, from the fourth belay anchor on a 15-pitch climb in the Canadian Rockies. After tumbling 115 feet, he came to rest on a ledge three pitches above the ground, having suffered only minor injuries. One might attribute this incident—especially when held opposite the equally implausible examples above—to benign intervention, a guidance bordering on the divine. Or one might say, it was merely good luck.

This book is filled with examples of good luck and bad—mainly the latter. But neither form of chance has anything to do with some alarming trends. Free solo deaths are becoming alarmingly frequent. Further on, you'll read of an unusual rescue of a stranded free soloist who had virtually no outdoor climbing experience.

Luck also plays no role in accidents that basic skills would have prevented. In this year's *ANAC* reporting, all 13 accidents caused by or aggravated by pulled protection involved failed cam placements. None of the pulled protection, whether placed by a novice or experienced climber, was a nut, hex, or Tricam. Like fast food, cams are fast, easy, and convenient. But a novice trad leader's diet should stress the use of passive gear to teach the basic principles of protection.

Finally, while the rallying cry of "Let's go!" may amp up the sheer optimism of the moment, it can drown out the faint whispers of prudence. Climbing draws a thin line between potential and peril. And for the inexperienced climber, magical thinking—a poor substitute for know-how and informed judgment—is too often applied to running it out to the chains, yarding on a creaky flake, or plodding upward into a snowstorm.

As an elective passion, climbing promises a glimpse of the unimaginable and the astounding—but please remember, these adjectives are also used when describing the aftermath of an accident. Considering it all, one might think that climbing is not a prudent pursuit—and one would be right. Climbing is not entirely prudent. It is beautiful and it is dangerous. Stay safe out there.

Submissions
Share your story and help fellow climbers. Visit *publications.americanalpineclub.org* to file an accident report or email us at *accidents@americanalpineclub.org*.

Friends of Accidents in North American Climbing
The following people and companies made donations specifically to support *ANAC*. Thank you! Show your support at *americanalpineclub.org/donate*.

Anonymous Supporters
Marcus Ariel
Dimitri Bevc
Jim Bodenhamer
Michael Brandt
Laura Chedalawada
John T. Cobb
Charlie Eiriksson
Carla Firey
Richard E. Hoffman, M.D.
Julian Kahn

Jeff Kilpatrick
Erich T. Koehler
Ryan Litwin
Scott Petersen
Steven Richards
Rocky Talkie
James Sneeringer
John Soebbing
Arthur Wang
Owen Zacharias

AAC RESCUE BENEFITS
Powered by Redpoint Travel Protection
Climbing can be a risky pursuit, but one well worth the price of admission. With our emergency rescue evacuation services and Medical Expense Benefit, you can tie in a little easier, knowing the Club has got your back. Some exclusions and limitations apply. Learn more at *americanalpineclub.org/rescue*. Partner-level AAC members and above receive:

$7,500 in Worldwide Emergency Rescue Evacuation Services
If disaster strikes, call Redpoint at *+1-628-251-1510* to be rescued and taken to the hospital. This coverage applies to any outdoor activity, other than flying, piloting, or acting as the crew of any aircraft. If you'll be traveling to more remote destinations, consider upgrading to the Leader-level membership to receive up to $300,000 in rescue coverage.

$5,000 in Medical Expense Coverage
During an eligible incident, your membership covers any direct medical expenses related to emergency stabilization that would otherwise be out of pocket.

Direct Expense Reimbursement
We created a reimbursement process so you're not left holding the bill in the event you are unable to initiate your rescue through Redpoint.

Additional Insurance Coverage
Planning a big trip this year? Consider Ripcord, Redpoint's comprehensive travel insurance. AAC members receive a 10% discount when they purchase further Redpoint travel programs—including comprehensive insurance for trip interruption/cancellation, baggage loss, search services, security evacuations, polar travel upgrades, and more. Visit *redpointtravelprotection.com /partner/aac* to learn more.

NPS rescue personnel and volunteers treat a HAPE/HACE patient at 14,200-foot camp on Denali. This portable and inflatable hyperbaric chamber is used to simulate emergent descent for severe cases of high altitude illness prior to evacuation or when descent is not possible. *Menno Boermans*

KNOW THE ROPES
MOUNTAIN MEDICINE

Acclimatization and High Altitude Illness: Assessment and Treatment
By Peter Hackett, M.D. & Dave Weber

High altitude illness (HAI) occurs when climbers are exposed to lower barometric pressure due to elevation gain. While ambient air is always composed of 21 percent oxygen, the less dense air at high altitude results in fewer available oxygen molecules and thus less oxygen in the lungs, blood, and tissues.

When a climber does not take adequate time to acclimatize to a new altitude, signs and symptoms (S/S) of HAI can manifest. The effects can range from mild to life-threatening. Early recognition and treatment are essential to minimize the severity of high altitude illness. The following recommendations are largely based on the 2024 update of the Wilderness Medical Society's (WMS) Consensus Guidelines for the Prevention and Treatment of Acute Altitude Illness.

Acclimatization
The human body can adjust to moderate hypoxia, reduced oxygen in the body tissues, at elevations less than 17,000 feet (5,182 meters) but requires time to do so. Acute

exposure to altitude is associated with a steady increase in ventilation (breathing rate and depth), improved oxygenation, and changes in cerebral (brain) blood flow. Later phases of acclimatization are marked by increased production of red blood cells (oxygen-carrying cells).

In general, high altitude illness affects climbers at sleeping elevations greater than 8,000 feet (2,438 meters). As the altitude increases, so does the risk of HAI. The rate of ascent, however, is the most important factor when assessing risk.

The WMS recommends avoiding ascents to a sleeping altitude of over 9,000 feet (2,743 meters) in one day from low altitude (less than 3,000 feet/914 meters) and increasing sleeping elevation by no more than 1,500 feet (~460 meters) per day when above 9,000 feet. In addition, the WMS guidelines recommend an extra day of acclimatization for every 3,000 feet of sleeping elevation gain. If a route requires larger elevation gains between camps, it is best to sleep at one elevation for two or more days while traveling to higher altitudes on day trips (hence the popular adage of "climb high and sleep low").

These recommendations are general, and the pace of acclimatization will be too slow for some and too fast for others. Climbers must pay attention to their bodies, and their partners, and recognize the early symptoms of altitude illness.

Under physician direction, the medication acetazolamide (Diamox) can be used to speed up the natural process of acclimatization and thus help prevent acute mountain sickness (AMS). Climbers at altitude should avoid consumption of products that depress their innate respiratory drive, such as sedative medications and alcoholic beverages.

Case Study

Failure to heed the HAI preventive measures listed above can have severe consequences. This point is highlighted in the unfortunate death of a 24-year-old male climber on Denali in 2023 (*see page 23*).

On May 30, National Park Service (NPS) mountaineering rangers at 14,200-foot camp (4,328 meters) were notified that a climber on an independent six-person ski-mountaineering team had repeatedly lost consciousness. His teammates informed the rangers that this climber appeared to be exhibiting signs and symptoms of high altitude cerebral edema (HACE) and high altitude pulmonary edema (HAPE), following a rapid, one-and-a-half-day ascent from Kahiltna Base Camp at 7,200 feet to 14,200-foot camp. The team also reported that a second climber on their team was exhibiting signs and symptoms of HAPE.

Poor weather prevented rapid evacuation by helicopter for the next 18 hours. The mountaineering rangers and their medical volunteers performed advanced life support measures throughout the night and for the duration of the weather hold. Treatments included a portable hyperbaric chamber, emergency HAI medications, supplemental oxygen, and mechanical breathing assistance. Despite these efforts, the climber never regained consciousness and remained unresponsive.

When the weather cleared on May 31, the NPS helicopter flew to 14,200-foot camp with a National Guard pararescue specialist aboard to evacuate the climber to Talkeetna. The climber was then flown via air ambulance to a hospital in Anchorage, where he died the following day as a result of severe high altitude illness.

This sobering incident underlines the necessity of adequate acclimatization during any high altitude expedition. Adding a few days to this team's ascent profile would have resulted in little or no HAI signs and symptoms for the climbers.

Assessment

High altitude illness encompasses three categories: acute mountain sickness (AMS), high altitude cerebral edema (HACE), and high altitude pulmonary edema (HAPE). Acute mountain sickness represents the mildest—and most common—form of high altitude illness. AMS is estimated to affect 25 percent of all visitors to Colorado who sleep above 8,000 feet, for example. HACE and HAPE are severe presentations of high altitude illness that are, fortunately, far less common.

AMS occurs when a non-acclimatized climber ascends to an altitude more rapidly than their body can adjust. The onset of AMS is usually within hours of ascent or after the first night of sleeping at altitude.

High altitude cerebral edema is severe AMS characterized by fluid accumulation (edema) within the brain—it usually takes two to three days to develop. The incidence of HACE is rare, especially at elevations below 14,000 feet (4,267 meters). HACE generally follows AMS or HAPE.

High altitude pulmonary edema is caused by excessive fluid leaking from capillaries within the lungs, and most often occurs two to three days after ascent to high altitude. HAPE is also uncommon and can occur by itself or in conjunction with AMS and HACE. Approximately one out of 10,000 skiers visiting Colorado and less than one out of 100 travelers above 14,000 feet (4,267 meters) suffer from HAPE.

Signs and Symptoms of High Altitude Illness

The following signs and symptoms are the most common presentations for each of the high altitude illnesses (AMS, HACE, and HAPE).

Acute Mountain Sickness

- Headache accompanied by at least one of the following:
  - Loss of appetite, nausea, and sometimes vomiting
  - Insomnia
  - Fatigue
  - Dizziness or lightheadedness
- Patients often report that AMS feels much like a hangover

High Altitude Cerebral Edema

- Ataxia (difficulties with coordination and gross motor movements, e.g., walking; patient may appear intoxicated)
- Mental status changes (including disorientation, irritability, combativeness, and/or unresponsiveness)
- Headache and other AMS signs and symptoms possible
- HAPE often present

High Altitude Pulmonary Edema

- Shortness of breath (respiratory distress) with exercise at first
- Shortness of breath when resting later
- Excessive fatigue
- Persistent cough (initially dry, then becoming productive)

Denali Rescue Volunteer Dr. Andy Luks assesses a HAPE patient in the NPS medical tent at 14,200-foot camp. *Menno Boermans*

- Gurgling sensation in the chest
- Very low pulse oximeter value (usually less than 70—80 percent, depending on the altitude)

Note: Pulse oximetry (SpO_2) monitors can be useful for monitoring an individual's oxygen saturation trend over time. However, persons with AMS can have normal values for the altitude, and many climbers with low values are not ill. That said, SpO_2 values are always low with HAPE. The normal value for a given altitude can be estimated by the average readings of well climbers in the group.

Field Treatment

The lists below highlight treatments that are both effective and practical in field settings. It is critical that any treatments recommended for AMS, HACE, and HAPE be realistic for typical high altitude mountain environments.

Acute Mountain Sickness

The most prudent treatment is to stop the ascent and allow the climber to acclimatize until S/S resolve. Rest days should be active while maintaining appropriate nutrition and hydration. In addition:

- Consider acetazolamide (Diamox).*
- Treat symptoms (e.g. headache, nausea) with over-the-counter medications.
- Supplemental oxygen can be administered if available.
- Descend if climber does not improve or if S/S of HACE/HAPE present.

High Altitude Cerebral Edema

The highest-priority treatment is prompt descent until S/S resolve. During descent:

- Supplemental oxygen should be administered if available.
- Administer dexamethasone (Decadron)* and continue until improvement with descent.
- A portable hyperbaric chamber can be used temporarily if descent is not possible.

High Altitude Pulmonary Edema

The highest-priority treatment is prompt descent until S/S resolve. During descent:

- Supplemental oxygen should be administerd if available.
- Consider inhaled albuterol (Ventolin).*
- Administer oral nifedipine (Procardia).*
- A portable hyperbaric chamber can be temporarily used if descent is not possible.

Note that HACE and HAPE can occur simultaneously, and differential diagnosis can prove difficult. For this reason, some experts recommend initially treating severe HAI patients with neurological S/S for both HACE and HAPE until a definitive diagnosis is established.

Hospital Treatment

Treatment of HAI in the hospital or clinic is similar to the field management strategies described above. Climbers suffering from HAI usually improve simply with transport to a lower elevation. HACE/HAPE patients should be assessed and monitored for any prolonged neurological and/or respiratory aftereffects.

*Administration of any medication requires both wilderness medicine training and physician orders/protocols.

*Peter Hackett is an M.D. researcher, climber, and expert on high altitude illness at the University of Colorado Anschutz Medical Campus. **Dave Weber** was a mountaineering ranger at Denali National Park for 13 seasons. He is the senior editor of ANAC, a climbing ranger at Grand Teton National Park, and a flight paramedic and hoist rescuer for Intermountain Life Flight.*

Avalanche First Aid
By Michael Buchanan & Dr. TJ Hartridge

I am Michael Buchanan. I am a flight paramedic with Intermountain Life Flight and co-founder of the After the Avalanche program (www.aftertheavalanche.org). My wife—an ICU nurse—and I recently attended a course reviewing safe travel in avalanche terrain, warning signs of avalanche, and how to perform avalanche companion rescue. These courses excel at teaching these aspects, but due to time constraints, they fail to delve into the realities of longer-term patient management following a successful rescue.

My curiosity on this topic led to additional self-study and revealed knowledge gaps regarding the morbidity of avalanche victims. An eagerness to close these gaps connected me with medical and avalanche professionals in Salt Lake City and Jackson, Wyoming. These subject matter experts—including physicians, SAR personnel, and avalanche forecasters—have spent decades researching avalanche morbidity. Their research includes common causes of avalanche-related death and practical first-aid treatments.

Avalanche Statistics
- The victim, or someone in their party, is the most common avalanche trigger.
- Most climber avalanche fatalities occur in spring and summer.
- Most forecasting uses an avalanche danger scale of "low," "moderate,"

Avalanche on Mt. Hunter in Denali National Park. While current avalanche courses cover safe travel, warning signs, and rescue, they often fail to address longer-term post-accident patient management. *Dave Weber*

"considerable," "high," and "extreme danger." Most fatalities occur when danger is "considerable."
- Most avalanches occur between 30 and 45 degrees.
- Many alpine climbing routes follow gully and couloir terrain features that create a funnel for avalanche slopes above. These "terrain traps" bury victims deeper than average.
- Two primary classifications: partial burial—where the victim is buried and their airway remains above the surface; complete/full burial—where the victim's airway is beneath the surface.
- The likelihood of surviving a partial avalanche burial is approximately 95 percent. The likelihood of surviving a complete/full burial is 50 percent.

Causes of Death

Three causes of death are commonly linked to avalanche fatalities: asphyxia, trauma, and hypothermia. Approximately 75 percent of avalanche fatalities are due to asphyxiation, 25 percent are trauma-related, and a small percentage are caused by hypothermia.

Asphyxia is a condition resulting from insufficient oxygen intake and can lead to death within 15 to 20 minutes. Three mechanisms cause asphyxiation: oxygen deprivation, airway blockage, and ice mask formation.

Oxygen Deprivation

Ambient air contains 21 percent oxygen and 0.04 percent carbon dioxide. Conversely, human exhalation contains 16 percent oxygen and 4 percent carbon dioxide. Avalanche debris has very little porosity and is not permeable to outside air. If an air pocket exists surrounding a buried victim, it quickly becomes enriched with carbon dioxide and depleted of oxygen during normal breathing. The continued rebreathing of this air mixture eventually causes asphyxiation due to hypoxia. This mechanism is the most common cause of avalanche deaths.

Airway Blockage

When a victim is entrained in an avalanche, their clothing, boots, and equipment are packed with snow. This phenomenon is also true of their airway, which includes the mouth and nose. As snow fills the oral and nasal cavities, it causes an impenetrable barrier to the passage of air into the lungs and leads to asphyxiation.

Ice Mask Formation

During inhalation of ambient air, the body humidifies dry air as a protective measure for upper airway structures and the lungs. During exhalation, the expired air contains water vapor. This water vapor is visible to climbers during winter months due to condensation of vapor in cold air. During an avalanche burial, exhaled water vapor condenses and freezes in front of the victim's airway. As this ice barrier develops, it prevents further inhalation and ultimately causes asphyxiation.

As mentioned, trauma accounts for nearly 25 percent of avalanche deaths. Multiple mechanisms of traumatic injury can occur during an avalanche. Avalanches can reach speeds greater than 60 mph (97 kph). Impacting terrain features, such as trees and rocks, at these speeds is a common cause of fatal trauma. Falling over cliff features is another means of traumatic injury when entrained in an avalanche. Trauma can cause death immediately or within 15 to 20 minutes of burial.

Common traumatic injuries involve the head, neck, chest, arms, and legs, with many victims having multiple body regions affected. These multi-system injuries are devastating and difficult to survive. Traumatic injuries can cause internal bleeding in the chest, abdomen, and head cavities. Traumatic brain injuries (TBI) are the most common type of head injury suffered. A TBI patient will commonly exhibit abnormal breathing patterns and have increased oxygen demands that may accelerate asphyxiation and further decrease chances of survival.

Hypothermia is responsible for a small percentage of avalanche deaths. In general, snow is a good insulator. (Climbers often experience this characteristic in the warmth of a snow cave.) In general, it takes burial of an hour, or longer, for a victim to become hypothermic. For this reason, asphyxia and trauma are more prevalent causes of death in the early stages of burial. Avalanche victims are more likely to asphyxiate before succumbing to hypothermia.

That said, hypothermia can complicate the compromised physiologic conditions of victims following a rescue. It represents one of the leading causes of death in typical trauma patients and should be managed during evacuation. Field treatments include providing warm and dry clothing to retain body heat and a vapor barrier (plastic bag, bivy sack, or tent fly) to protect the victim from wind and precipitation.

Although this is anecdotal, climbers could be more susceptible to trauma as a cause of death versus snowmobilers, skiers, and snowboarders. The narrow confines that characterize climbing routes can compound the effects of even a small avalanche, exposing victims to trees, rocks, and deeper burials. This possibility was highlighted in the tragic avalanche accident in February 2023 that killed three out of six climbers ascending the tight, rocky chute of the Northeast Couloir of Colchuck Peak in Washington (*see page 89*). Three of the four climbers caught in the slide were not buried, but died from traumatic injuries.

Companion Rescue

There is a short survivability window for any avalanche victim. Most avalanche fatalities are caused by asphyxiation, so it is essential to locate and recover victims within 15 to 20 minutes of burial. Efficient companion rescue skills are the difference between life and death. Backcountry travelers should not rely on SAR teams. The odds of successful professional rescue are very low, given the hours required to mobilize.

Avalanche First Aid

Numerous resources exist for current best practices including the International Commission on Alpine Rescue (ICAR) guidelines and the Wilderness Medical Society (WMS) Consensus Guidelines. However, some of that information is directed at advanced medical practitioners or environments with a more robust helicopter rescue system. For simplified recommendations, please refer to the Avalanche First Aid Algorithm chart (*see above*).

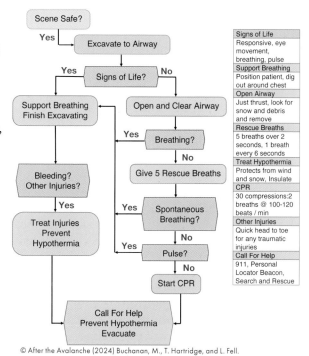

© After the Avalanche (2024) Buchanan, M., T. Hartridge, and L. Fell.

After the Avalanche offers simplified and unified recommendations for non—medical professionals and rescuers, responding to an avalanche accident. © *After the Avalanche*

When rescuing any avalanche victim, the priority should be exposing the head and chest as quickly as possible. Many rescue drills incorrectly focus on exposing the victim's head. Unfortunately, as long as the chest remains buried, adequate respiration and ventilation are nearly impossible.

After exposing the head and the chest, the victim should be assessed for signs of life. This is typically referred to as an initial patient assessment, or the ABC's (Airway, Breathing, Circulation). The following is a list of considerations during the initial assessment:

- Is the victim responding spontaneously to voice commands or painful stimulus?
- Is the victim spontaneously opening her/his eyes?
- Is the victim's airway clear of snow?
- Is the victim breathing spontaneously?
- Does the victim have a pulse?
- What color are the victim's lips, mouth, and face?

If a victim is breathing and responding when found, complete their excavation in order to assess for traumatic injuries to the head, neck, spine, chest, abdomen, pelvis, and extremities. Rescuers should be proactive with management of hypothermia. Practically, this means providing warm and dry clothing to the victim, in addition to layers that protect from wind and precipitation. If additional help is required, rescue personnel can be notified by calling 911 or sending an emergency satellite message.

If there are no signs of life (unresponsive, not breathing, no pulse), manually clear the airway of any snow/debris. Once cleared, the airway should be opened using the jaw thrust or head tilt—chin lift maneuver, as taught in a first-aid class.

If the victim is breathing, rescuers should support breathing, finish the excavating process, treat for hypothermia, and plan for evacuation. If the victim is not breathing, deliver five rescue breaths. Ideally, a pocket mask should be used, but, if not, mouth-to-mouth resuscitation is an option. Each rescue breath should last one to two seconds or until chest rise is observed. Each breath should be given six seconds apart. If the victim begins to breathe spontaneously after these initial breaths, support breathing and continue the patient assessment.

If no spontaneous breathing occurs after these initial rescue breaths, check for a pulse for ten seconds or less. The preferred site is the carotid artery, which is located on the neck, below the jaw, and on either side of the trachea/windpipe. If no pulse is felt, begin cardiopulmonary resuscitation (CPR).

Begin CPR by performing 30 chest compressions at a rate of 100 to 120 compressions per minute. A metronome phone application set at 110 beats per minute can help maintain proper cadence. The American Heart Association (AHA) recommends giving two rescue breaths after each round of 30 chest compressions. Five cycles of 30 compressions and two breaths should be completed before briefly reassessing (ten seconds or less) for the return of spontaneous breathing and/or a pulse.

If a victim is responsive, breathing and has a pulse, they should be thoroughly assessed for traumatic injuries. Initial assessment can be as simple as asking the victim if anything hurts. Palpate (feel) the entire body and note any abnormalities or areas of pain or tenderness. Spinal injury should be assumed on all unresponsive victims and efforts should be made to minimize movement of their head, neck, and spine. Once the physical examination is complete, basic first-aid treatments such as bandaging and splinting can be addressed while waiting for additional help or preparing for evacuation.

Withholding or Discontinuing Medical Care

There are scenarios where first aid will not help an avalanche victim and efforts should be withheld. If a scene is unsafe for rescuers, do not initiate rescue and/or escape to a safe zone and call for additional help. If there are obvious fatal injuries or the victim is completely frozen, first aid should not be initiated. If the victim was buried longer than 60 minutes, the airway is blocked with snow/debris, and the body is cold, the victim has likely died from asphyxia.

If CPR has been in progress for greater than 30 minutes and no signs of life are present, CPR can be terminated. One exception to this time limit for CPR is for potential hypothermia victims. In the field, this is demarked by a burial longer than 60 minutes and an airway clear of snow/debris when found. Unlike for asphyxia and trauma victims, hypothermia treatment should be continued until rescue personnel arrive, due to higher survivability potential.

Psychological First Aid

Involvment in an avalanche, as either a victim or a rescuer, can cause traumatic psychological stress, often with lasting effects. Psychological injuries often go unrecognized and untreated. These stress injuries have the potential to alter the lives of victims and rescuers alike. It is important for anyone involved in an avalanche to be familiar with and recognize these stressors. Laura McGladrey wrote an excellent article addressing the traumatic stress injuries in *ANAC 2019*. Baseline information and proven tactics were presented in this article.

Education

Travel in avalanche terrain carries inherent risks. Continuing education is recommended to stay practiced and apprised of avalanche avoidance, rescue techniques, and medical care. Climbers and skiers should seek out courses reviewing terrain recognition and companion rescue methodology. Additionally, basic first aid and CPR rounds out the skills necessary to rescue partners. The American Heart Association and the American Red Cross offer courses. Wilderness-specific medical courses are a step above these introductory trainings.

Conclusion

When venturing into avalanche terrain, climbers, skiers, and companions are the best rescue resource when an accident occurs. The best means of rescuing an avalanche victim is to find them efficiently and utilize baseline avalanche rescue tools (transceiver, probe, and shovel). Avalanche first aid encompasses many techniques covered in basic first-aid and CPR classes. The Avalanche First Aid Algorithm can aid rescuers in low-frequency, high-consequence rescues, and in patient assessments required for the recovery and resuscitation of victims. Because avalanches pose a risk to anyone venturing into snowy environments, it is essential to maintain one's skills in avalanche awareness, companion rescue, first aid, and survival.

Michael J. Buchanan, NRP, FP-C, FAWM, is a flight paramedic with Intermountain Life Flight and co-founder of the After the Avalanche program. He is an avid backcountry skier, and rock and ice climber. Theodore "TJ" Hartridge, D.O., FAWM, is a longtime ski patroller in Colorado and Utah. He is an emergency medicine physician in Utah and Wyoming and co-founder of the After the Avalanche program.

Relevant Literature

- "2024 Wilderness Medical Society Practice Guidelines for Prevention and Management of Avalanche and Nonavalanche Snow Burial Accidents"
- "2019 Wilderness Medical Society Clinical Practice Guidelines for the Out-of-Hospital Evaluation and Treatment of Accidental Hypothermia"
- "2019 Wilderness Medical Society Clinical Practice Guidelines for Spinal Cord Protection"

Andrea Bender climbing Misty (5.10b/c), the scene of the fatal fall of Yutung Zhang in October 2023. *Andrea Bender Collection*

ALABAMA

FATAL FALL FROM ANCHOR | Inexperience, Inadequate Supervision
Alabama, Sand Rock, Sun Wall

On October 14, Yutung "Faye" Zhang (18) fell 90 feet from the anchors of Misty (5.10b/c) while preparing to clean this route at Sand Rock in northeastern Alabama. It was her second time climbing outdoors. At around 12 p.m., Zhang, a new climber and part of a larger group, took a final top-rope lap on the route. She cleaned the quickdraws and reached the two-bolt anchor. The anchor was equipped with two mussy hooks plus a single locking carabiner that had been placed by one of the other climbers to prevent the rope from unclipping from the mussies.

No one was at the anchors with Zhang to see exactly what happened. June C, who was belaying Zhang at the time of the accident, wrote on Mountain Project, "We put the locker in on the incredibly unlikely premise that the mussys could come unclipped. Not that any of us really thought that would happen, but we wanted to keep our party safe. [While Zhang was on the ground], we communicated and demonstrated what she was to do when she got to the top and she was aware and confident of just needing to remove a locker and leave the mussys clipped."

It is assumed that after removing the locking carabiner at the belay, Zhang somehow unclipped the rope from the mussy hooks. Jun C wrote, "Suddenly the rope became unweighted and she wasn't clipped through the [hooks] anymore. I fell and smacked my back and head against another rock and she fell right beside me.... A few of us trained in emergency first response came to aid immediately as well as a physician that just happened to be in the area. EMS response was quite fast as well but there was really nothing to be done."

June C added, "Between all of us we have decades of climbing experience. In our eyes, this [lowering from the mussy hooks] was routine and one of the safest things we could ask of a relatively new climber." The belayer added, "At the same time I know all of us are kicking ourselves for asking her to do anything at all.... We've all been thinking about what we could or should have done differently or how this could have been a safer experience."

ANALYSIS

A few weeks after the accident, IFMGA guide Karsten Delap climbed the route and provided *ANAC* with some images and video. He observed that the best handholds at the end of Misty were located above the bolts. This may have positioned Zhang above the mussy hooks. Then, as Zhang weighted the rope, it might have loaded the hooks incorrectly and become unclipped.

Delap wrote, "It is plausible that the rope was threaded from right to left on the mussy hooks, with the locking carabiner positioned between the two hooks. As the climber approached the anchor from the right side, an attempt to remove the locking carabiner involved pulling up above the mussy hooks to introduce slight slack into the system. While this facilitated the removal of the carabiner, it also inadvertently positioned the rope over the gates of the mussy hooks. The belayer, responding to the climber's movement, probably took up slack, felt the climber's weight, and subsequently the gates of the mussy hooks back-clipped under the full force of the climber's weight. This resulted in the rope becoming dislodged from the anchor."

Delap also noted that the addition of a locking carabiner to this mussy hook belay was inappropriate for the system. In this case, the locker brought the rope above the plane of the hooks, a mistake when considering the "open" nature of a mussy hook. (*See "Essentials" on the next page.*)

Greg Barnes, executive director of the American Safe Climbing Association (ASCA), is a proponent of lower-offs such as mussy hooks, but he says these useful tools still require education. He wrote to *ANAC*, "In Owens River Gorge, lower-offs [have been] the standard since the early '90s. Despite very heavy climber traffic for 30 years, there have been very few anchor changeover accidents compared to similar areas with closed anchors. In the Sand Rock case, we don't know whether the rope became accidentally unclipped or if the climber unclipped them on purpose. It is wise to have direct supervision—namely an experienced climber at the same anchor—when a new climber cleans an anchor." (*Sources: MountainProject.com, Climbing.com, Karsten Delap, Greg Barnes, and the Editors.*)

ESSENTIALS

MUSSY HOOKS: BE A PRO, KEEP IT LOW
By Karsten Delap, IFMGA Guide

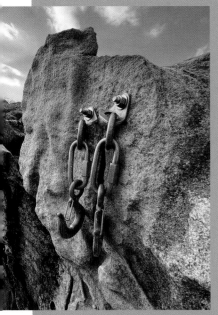

The anchor at the top of Misty at Sand Rock, Alabama. Karsten Delap, a guide who visited the area after a fatal accident in October (see previous pages), said, "When she... undid the [locking] carabiner...she was probably a little bit above [the hooks], with a little bit of slack." Be a pro, keep it low. *Karsten Delap*

Mussy hooks, also known as open anchor hardware or lower-offs, have been used for decades at various single-pitch climbing areas. This type of anchor point not only makes it easy for a climber to clip and lower, but also provides sustainability for high-traffic areas due to the hardware's durability.

Mussy hooks have non-locking gates and, for various reasons, are usually installed so the gates face the same direction. This creates the potential for "back-clipping" to happen if the climber or rope is somehow positioned above the hooks. This also makes mussy hooks less than ideal for numerous climbers to use in a top-rope setting, because a slack rope with twists could unclip from the hooks. This scenario is very unlikely, but not impossible.

For those using mussy hooks in a top-rope setting, the recommended practice is to establish an anchor with a masterpoint below the plane of the hooks. When the last climber goes to clean the hooks, they will reach up to clip the rope above the temporary anchor into the hooks, then have the belayer take. All the climber's weight will then be on the hooks and should be tested in a manner that confirms this; this also should unweight the temporary anchor, making it easy to clean.

If the climber cannot unweight the rope from the temporary anchor, a PAS (personal anchor system) can be attached to the masterpoint of that anchor to hold the weight of the climber while they transfer the rope to the hooks. In either case, a key to safety is to position the temporary anchor low, so the climber cleaning the anchor must lift the rope up to clip the mussy hooks.

Whenever possible, the best practice when using mussy hooks is to ensure that your harness tie-in points, any temporary anchors, and the rope all stay below the mussy hooks until you're ready to lower. So be a pro, keep it low.

It is strongly discouraged for inexperienced climbers to attempt to clean a route without proper and direct supervision. Many preventable accidents have occurred when inexperienced climbers clean a route for the first time. The safest and most effective way to learn this crucial skill is through the guidance of a certified instructor or guide in a controlled learning environment, where the progression of skills can be tailored to the individual climber's needs.

Denali is the highest peak in North America. The name, derived from the Native Alaskan Koyukon language, means "the tall one." High latitude and other factors make its 20,310-foot summit about 1000 feet physiologically higher than the same altitude in the Himalayas. *NPS | Tim Rains*

ALASKA

DENALI NATIONAL PARK ACCIDENT SUMMARY

National Park Service (NPS) mountaineering rangers treated a total of 33 patients during the 2023 climbing season in the Alaska Range. The following list provides a breakdown of the diagnoses. (*Some patients had multiple diagnoses.*)

- *Traumatic Injury:* 11 cases (includes one facial laceration, three shoulder injuries, one traumatic brain injury, one case of fractured ribs, one neck injury, and four patients with various musculoskeletal injuries)
- *Frostbite:* 11 cases
- *Medical:* Six cases (includes two cases of hypothermia, one diverticulitis, one spontaneous pneumothorax, one possible case of anxiety, and one case of anaphylaxis)
- *High Altitude Cerebral Edema (HACE):* Three cases
- *High Altitude Pulmonary Edema (HAPE):* Three cases

Twenty-one patients required helicopter evacuation from Denali National Park. Three patients were evacuated by NPS rangers on the ground, and nine patients self-evacuated after receiving treatment.

There were three mountaineering-related deaths in the Alaska Range during the 2023 climbing season, with an additional post-evacuation fatality. One occurred when a solo skier was caught in an avalanche. Two fatalities occurred due to a fall from the Mooses Tooth in the Ruth Gorge. On Denali's West Buttress, a climber suffering from severe altitude illness was treated and evacuated, but subsequently died in hospital. (*See individual reports below.*)

While some accidents are difficult to predict and prevent, many of the medical illnesses and traumatic injuries are preventable with prudent decision-making and a reasonable ascent profile during climbing expeditions. Additional information regarding the prevention, recognition, and treatment of common mountain medicine maladies can be found at the Denali National Park website: search "Denali mountaineering medical issues." *(Source: Denali Mountaineering Rangers.)*

UNROPED CREVASSE FALL
Denali, West Buttress Route

On May 17, a 43-year-old female climber fell into a crevasse while unroped on Motorcycle Hill, above 11,200-foot camp. This climber was ascending without skis or snowshoes at the time of the fall. She was assisted out of the crevasse by one of her teammates and another private climber. The climber fell over 15 feet until stopping at the crevasse bottom and sustained a dislocated shoulder in the process. The dislocation was successfully reduced, and the patient was transported by helicopter to 7,200-foot base camp once the weather cleared.

ANALYSIS

The year 2023 marks the third year in a row that NPS personnel have responded to an unroped crevasse fall in the Alaska Range. This year, the patient was fortunate. The crevasse falls in 2021 and 2022 proved fatal. The only sure way to mitigate crevasse fall hazard is by traveling as part of a rope team. While the use of a rope will not prevent a fall from occurring, it will reduce the fall distance and the likely severity of injury. Also, a means of floatation, such as skis or snowshoes, may reduce fall potential by distributing the weight of a climber over a greater surface area.

An unroped crevasse fall not only is risky for the individual, but also for other climbers. Most of these incidents are responded to and resolved by bystanders, not by professional rescuers. Climbers should consider this trend and assess their companion rescue plan prior to embarking on glaciated travel. *(Source: Denali Mountaineering Rangers.)*

UNROPED FALL WHILE DESCENDING
Denali, West Buttress Route

At approximately 11 p.m. on May 19, a 24-year-old male climber was descending the ridge below 17,200-foot camp when he fell roughly 1,200 vertical feet onto the Peters Glacier. He and his climbing partner had just summited via the West Rib and were descending back to 14,200-foot camp. The fallen climber's partner reported they were a few minutes from the fixed lines, at 16,200 feet, when the fall occurred. The partner was able to see the fallen climber on the Peters Glacier but was unable to make verbal contact. Due to the steep, crevassed terrain below the ridge, the partner made the decision to descend to 14,200-foot camp and notify NPS personnel.

Poor weather at the time of notification prevented helicopter evacuation, and a ground rescue was initiated. Due to the challenging access and remote nature of the patient's location, the ground response team was prepared to spend an extended period of time on the scene. However, the weather eventually cleared, allowing helicopter extrication 20 hours after the fall. The patient sustained a closed head injury and extensive frostbite on both hands.

The ridge on the West Buttress Route between the top of the fixed lines, at 16,200 feet, and 17,200-foot camp has been the site of many falls. These have resulted in multiple injuries and fatalities. Guide services and the NPS maintain running protection in areas of high exposure along the ridge. However, the non-technical terrain has lured many into bypassing the running protection to move faster or to pass other parties. It is understandable that after completing a more technical route with higher exposure, like the

Though the West Buttress is considered a "walk-up" in technical terms, it offers plenty of steep climbing. Bypassing fixed lines such as these, located below 16,200 feet, puts other climbers and rescuers in danger. *Dave Weber*

West Rib, climbers may be more focused on returning to camp than taking added precautions. While this accident had a positive outcome, it could have easily ended in tragedy. *(Source: Denali Mountaineering Rangers.)*

HIGH ALTITUDE CEREBRAL EDEMA | Ascending Too Fast
Denali, West Buttress Route

On May 30, an independent expedition at 14,200-foot camp notified rangers via radio that one member of their team, a 24-year-old Coloradan, had an altered mental status. The patient's team stated that they had been dropped off by plane at base camp (7,200 feet) on May 27. Immediately upon landing, the team departed via the West Buttress Route, reaching 14,200-foot camp a day and a half later, on the evening of May 28. The team stated that upon reaching camp, all team members were feeling "okay."

On the afternoon of May 30, teammates alerted NPS rangers that the Coloradan—after reportedly feeling "groggy" with a slight headache—began exhibiting severe symptoms of high altitude cerebral edema (HACE) and high altitude pulmonary edema (HAPE). A second team member was experiencing moderate symptoms of HAPE.

Weather conditions did not allow helicopter flights on the night of May 30. A team of NPS rangers and volunteer patrol members performed 18 hours of advanced life support on the unresponsive HACE/HAPE patient throughout the night, including treatment in a hyperbaric chamber, medications, supplemental oxygen, and mechanical breathing assistance. On the morning of May 31, the patient was evacuated by helicopter, with an Air National Guard pararescue specialist from the 212th Rescue Squadron serving as the medical attendant. The patient was flown to Talkeetna and transferred to a LifeMed air ambulance for advanced care. Unfortunately, the patient succumbed to the effects of HACE/HAPE in the hospital.

As many do, this team made the assumption that living at a relatively high altitude (over 5,000 feet) and maintaining a high level of fitness would prepare them adequately for swift elevation gain. This is a severe example of the inaccuracies of this assumption. Living at altitude and having good fitness are not guaranteed to protect climbers against high altitude illness (HAI). The human body starts losing adaptions to altitude in a matter of days, which is often the amount of time that climbers spend traveling to Alaska to begin an expedition.

The Wilderness Medical Society (WMS) recommends that, at elevations above 9,000 feet, climbers ascend no more than 1,650 feet (500 meters) to a new sleeping elevation each night. Additionally, for every 3,300 feet (1,000 meters) of elevation gain, the WMS recommends spending an extra day sleeping at a given elevation to further acclimatize. (*For more information on proper acclimatization, see the Know the Ropes article on page 8.*)

The mountaineering rangers on Denali see many very fit climbers arriving to attempt a summit each season. Although fitness is an important factor in risk management and safe travel on the mountain, it can also make the recommended conservative ascent profile feel onerous. Unfortunately, a climber's level of fitness has no correlation with whether they become stricken with HAI. Only a reasonable ascent profile and proper acclimatization will prevent climbers from becoming ill. *(Source: Denali Mountaineering Rangers.)*

STRANDED | Frostbite
Denali, West Buttress Route

At approximately 10 a.m. on June 7, I (Jonathan Gopel, 31), Jacob Dong (21), and Heath Himstedt (37) began descending from 17,200-foot camp on the West Buttress. Bad weather and extreme cold played into our decision to descend without a summit. We appeared to be the first party to leave 17,200-foot camp that morning. We descended the ridge to the top of the fixed lines at 16,200 feet as quickly as conditions permitted, as it was windy and very cold and we were looking to get below the cloud layer to find better conditions.

As we reached the top of the fixed lines, we came upon a party of two mountaineers who signaled to us that they needed assistance. We made a brief assessment, and it was clear they were not going to be able to descend the fixed lines without help. At this point, I activated the SOS feature on my Garmin inReach and began trying to communicate with rescuers while Heath, a trained Wilderness First Responder, assessed that one of the distressed mountaineers, Climber 1, was suffering from frostbite in his hands and potentially on his nose. He was nearly hypothermic. The other distressed mountaineer, Climber 2, seemed fine physically, but mentally he seemed somewhat disconnected and potentially suffering from altitude sickness. He required instructions on how to complete basic tasks. We decided our priorities would be keeping Climber 1 as warm as possible, while keeping an eye on Climber 2 while we awaited assistance.

It was taking up to 15 minutes to send or receive each message on the inReach due to the weather and our location. We decided it might be faster to have Jacob descend to 14,200-foot camp and report directly to the rangers. We knew this decision was somewhat risky, as there is some crevasse hazard below the fixed lines. But we decided it was worthwhile since there was a well-established bootpack and we were familiar with the terrain. Additionally, from where we were positioned, we would be able to watch Jacob's descent.

While we waited for a rescue, we got out sleeping bags and parkas and bundled Heath and Climber 1 together to share warmth. As another party descending from 17,200-foot camp offered help, I saw a team of two climbers below, moving towards the fixed lines. I thought this might be the rangers. Hoping to keep the scene clear, I suggested that the descending party continue going down; they left us with a bivy bag that we used to additionally shelter Climber 1.

After two hours, the wind shifted and we made the difficult decision to move Climber 1 up the hill to a more sheltered area. With an anchored belay, we essentially dragged him to the new location, a few hundred feet away. After approximately an hour, the two climbers I had seen ascending arrived at the top of the fixed lines. They were not the rangers, but one was a retired guide. He took the lead on the rescue.

As a group, we decided to lower Climber 1 down the fixed lines. We had a 60m half rope that we attached to his harness. I lowered Climber 1 down the fixed lines from above while others descended alongside. Getting him down the fixed lines took 60 to 90 minutes. As we were nearing the bottom, the initial ranger response arrived. The rangers took over, and Climber 1 was taken to the medical tent at 14,200-foot camp.

ANALYSIS

I believe my team made good choices throughout this rescue. We were quick to act and constantly reevaluated our decisions to fit the changing circumstances. We were lucky that Climber 1 was already in his harness, as getting him into it would have been difficult.

It would have been wise to have the descending party that left the bivy bag stay with us in case extra help was needed. At the time, we did not recognize that things had the potential to go downhill the way they started to. I don't think having extra people around a rescue is ever a detriment, as long as the rescue is being managed well and it doesn't create a bystander effect. We received good feedback from NPS rangers about the incident. *(Source: Jonathan Gopel.)*

AVALANCHE | Fatal Climbing Fall
Ruth Gorge, Mooses Tooth

On May 7, Eli Michel (34) and Nafiun Awal (32) were reported overdue to NPS personnel in Talkeetna, Alaska. The team had been camping in the Ruth Gorge with a primary climbing objective of the West Ridge of the Mooses Tooth (10,335 feet). The West Ridge (5,200 feet, 60°) is a classic mountaineering route that

DENALI PRO AWARDS

DENALI PRO AWARD

In the incident involving two stranded climbers near the top of the fixed lines at 16,200 feet (see page 24), Jacob Dong, Jonathan Gopel, and Heath Himstedt rendered critical aid to fellow climbers who were facing a life-and-death emergency.

For exemplary expedition behavior, these three along with teammate Amit Sule (who was in camp on the day of the rescue) were recognized with the Denali Pro lapel pin. Each climbing season, Denali mountaineering rangers grant this award for protecting the mountain environment, assisting fellow climbers, and using good judgment to limit or eliminate injury.

MISLOW-SWANSON DENALI PRO AWARD

At season's end, Denali rangers also select one or more Mislow-Swanson Denali Pro Award winners from the pin recipients.

This recognition program honors the memory of John Mislow and Andrew Swanson, who won the award for exemplary climbing ethics during the 2000 climbing season. The two men tragically died on the West Rib in 2009. The Mislow and Swanson families have worked with Denali National Park to create a special donation to honor the men and ensure the continuation of the program.

2023 AWARD WINNERS

Throughout the 2023 climbing season, mountain guides on Denali continued to work alongside NPS climbing staff on numerous search and rescues. Denali mountaineering staff want to recognize the following guides with the 2023 Mislow-Swanson Denali Pro Award.

(L to R) Himstedt, Gopel, and Dong preparing to climb up to 17,200-foot camp. While descending two days later, they came to the aid of two distressed climbers just above the saddle at the top left of this photo. Barely visible are teams of climbers ascending fixed lines below the saddle. *Amit Sule*

Will Gordon, of the American Alpine Institute, was notified on June 15 of a climbing accident in 17,200-foot camp. For the next ten hours, Gordon and his guide team provided the patient with medical care and transportation to a helicopter extraction location. They also provided care for the injured climber's team.

Sam Hennessey, of Alpine Ascents Denali, and **Michael Gardner**, from the Alaska Mountaineering School, both worked with NPS rangers to transport rescue gear to the 16,200-foot ridge on Denali's West Buttress. This was part of a complex rescue of a climber who had fallen from the 16,200-foot ridge to the Peters Glacier on May 19 (see page 22).

Gardner, along with his guide team, also assisted climbers suffering from altitude illness at 17,200-foot camp. They provided care for the distressed climbers until an NPS ranger patrol arrived. *(Source: Denali Mountaineering Rangers.)*

has fallen out of favor in recent years due to the increased popularity of more direct and technical lines to the summit, including Ham and Eggs and Shaken, Not Stirred. Throughout their trip, the climbers had been checking in daily with a friend. Their final communication was on May 5 and stated that they were departing on the climb.

Following the overdue notification on May 7, NPS personnel were able to conduct a helicopter reconnaissance. After locating the overdue climbers' camp, the personnel onboard the aircraft were able to clearly identify and follow the climbers' approach and ascent track up the West Ridge.

The team had cached skis and other gear on the ridge at the point where the climbing became more technical and a transition to crampons was required. The final observed tracks ascended the ridge at approximately 9,200 feet. These tracks terminated at the crown of a small avalanche in terrain with slope angles less than 50°. Below the avalanche crown, the terrain is comprises 3,000 feet of complex and crevassed alpine features. Both aerial and ground searches continued for 12 days after the initial report. Unfortunately, these searches only yielded sightings of scattered gear. NPS personnel concluded the fall and the exposure were not survivable, and rescue efforts ultimately were terminated.

The West Ridge of the Mooses Tooth is a long snow and ice route featuring ice up to 60° and long expanses of steep snow. The snow section marked above was the site of an avalanche that caused the death of two climbers in May 2023. *Brian Sterling | Wikimedia*

ANALYSIS

Many details surrounding this accident remain unknown. It is unclear whether the climbers were roped together or utilizing running protection. A small avalanche with significant exposure to steep terrain can have tragic consequences. This is true even in circumstances where the slide originates in benign terrain. Even for a competent and experienced team such as these climbers, isolated pockets of wind slab or storm slab can be difficult to predict. Climbers must be attentive to the terrain they are traveling in as well as the consequences of falling into the terrain below.

This incident also highlights the benefits of carrying and communicating via two-way satellite devices on climbing expeditions. This team had scheduled check-ins with a reliable friend. This strategy allowed for efficient notification of emergency personnel and led to a timely resolution of the incident. *(Sources: Denali Mountaineering Rangers and the AP.)*

ARIZONA

KNEE STUCK IN CRACK
Sedona, Queen Victoria Spire

On January 8, Climber 1 (female 25) got her knee stuck in a wide crack on the Regular Route (3 pitches, 5.7) on Queen Victoria Spire in Sedona. Climber 1 was following four friends on her first outdoor climb when she attempted an "alpine knee" while pulling onto a ledge on the second pitch. An "alpine knee" is when you place that joint on top of a high hold and use it for progress, instead of a foot. Rather than helping her onto the ledge, Climber 1's knee slipped into a four-inch-wide crack, where it wedged and became stuck. Others in her party tried pouring water over her knee in an attempt to free it but were unsuccessful.

At 5:15 p.m., the Coconino County Sheriff's department was contacted to perform a rescue. By 8 p.m., the SAR team had arrived. It took over an hour to free the climber from the crack, and by then the climber was exhibiting signs of mild hypothermia (they had started climbing at 12:30 p.m.). The climbing party was airlifted off the spire. The stuck climber was not injured and refused treatment.

ANALYSIS

The climbers in this scenario did "everything right," according to the SAR team. They tried to free their partner, and when they couldn't, they initiated a rescue. Many relatively easy routes have awkward sections or styles of climbing that may seem above the technical grade when first encountered outdoors. Care should be taken when making a move where a slip or fall could result in injury or entrapment. It took about four hours to free this climber, and temperatures at the crag dropped to around 30°F. Consider worst-case scenarios when preparing for a climb, as unexpected events could result in prolonged exposure to the elements. *(Source: Dan Apodaca.)*

UNROPED FALL | Loose Rock
Prescott, Granite Dells, Corndog Wall

On September 17, my boyfriend, Adam, my son, Tyler, our friends Chase and Megan, and I, Melissa Wright, were climbing at the Corndog Wall. Adam was at the top of a route, giving a refresher to Megan on cleaning an anchor. I was at the bottom. We saw two climbers approach with a crash pad. To my knowledge, there were no bouldering routes on our wall, so our assumption was they would move on. The young men were part of a large group who attended nearby Embry-Riddle Aeronautical University. The rest of their group—at least eight more—were sport climbing nearby.

Adam saw one of the guys free solo up a 20-foot-high rock face to our right. The area where they were climbing had no established routes listed on Mountain Project. As the guy started downclimbing, Adam yelled to him that there was an easy walk-off. The young man said he was fine and that the walk-off was too far.

Once the first guy was down, his friend "Bill," began to climb. He also was unroped. "Bill" was wearing a bike helmet, and we later discovered this was roughly

The scene of the rockfall accident at the Granite Dells. Note the crushed crash pad and shattered debris. The rocks were dislodged by a climber from the area on the cliff marked by the yellow box. To give a sense of scale, the figure in the red jacket is six feet, two inches tall. *Melissa Wright*

his third time climbing. I heard the sound of a massive rockfall, followed by screaming. "Bill" appeared to have been holding on to a large block that pulled out.

We called 911. I came up to the scene and saw "Bill" sitting upright. There was a large boulder sitting on the crash pad along with a scattering of smaller rocks. I saw blood on the wall, and I could see all the muscle and bone in his left calf. His right femur was broken, and he was missing most of the skin on the backside of his thigh. I ran to my pack and grabbed my first-aid kit and some clothing to treat the wounds, as it was obvious the gauze we had would not be enough. Adam made his way down, evaluated the scene, deemed it safe from further rockfall, put on gloves, and began applying pressure to "Bill's" wounds.

After speaking with rescue services, I gave the young guys a task to cover every entrance and junction to guide the EMTs, as it was unclear what route they would take. It only took 20 minutes for the EMTs to arrive.

ANALYSIS

Crowding, loose rock, unroped climbing on new terrain, inexperience—all these factors played into an accident that was easily avoidable.

Wright also notes, "Their first-aid kits were inadequate and two of them offered tourniquets. They wanted to move 'Bill' into shade. Based on the severity of his injuries, moving him could have severed an artery. It's one of the few times I didn't have my Garmin. I never adventure without it now." *(Source: Melissa Wright.)*

The rough approach to Table Dome played a factor in the call for rescue after Steve Sagin took a long leader fall on Wily Javelina. His partner, Jerry Cagle, wrote, "The topography is generally rugged and invariably involves some degree of bushwhacking." *Jerry Cagle*

FALL ON ROCK | Broken Hold
Mendoza Canyon, Table Dome

On February 24, Steve Sagin (58) and Jerry Cagle (70) were climbing Wily Javelina (6 pitches, 5.9 PG-13) on Table Dome in the remote Mendoza Canyon, southwest of Tucson. On pitch five, Sagin broke a hold and took a long leader fall.

Cagle wrote to *ANAC*:

Wily Javelina is a coveted route and considered a bit of a testpiece. Though it's frequently climbed using just the bolts, the distances between them are considerable; they can be supplemented with gear—albeit possibly dubious—so we also carried a light rack. We each carried cell phones, and I carried a Garmin inReach Mini. We had jackets, space blankets, food, water, and headlamps.

Reaching the start of the approach hike entails driving for 9.5 miles on an unmaintained dirt road. The approach wends through two miles of rugged trails. The areas adjacent to the paths present an impenetrable barrier of catclaw acacias and thorny mesquite trees.

It was around 10 a.m. when we started climbing. Steve led pitch one, with the first bolt 30 to 40 feet off the ground. We swung leads. Though I had always shied away from this route due to its reputation for serious runouts and sections of poor-quality rock, neither of us was excessively nervous. But throughout the course of the climb, we repeated the mantra that "falling was not an option." It is my considered opinion that this route is the textbook definition of an R-rated route and not PG-13 (as graded on Mountain Project).

As Steve led pitch five, he passed the middle mark on the ropes (60m x 7.9mm twin/half ropes). He was well past the second bolt on the "chicken-head-studded" upper section, at the start of the easier climbing, when a large hold fractured, sending considerable debris past my helmet. He fell and struck a large ledge 30 or 40 feet below him with the full force of his weight. The rope came taut as he started to slide off the ledge. It was immediately obvious that he was seriously injured.

We determined that lowering him to my position at the anchor was our best option. We had enough rope to lower him to the stance with about ten feet to spare.

Steve was bleeding in several places but not excessively. His broken ankle was likely the most serious injury, and we determined it was not a compound [open] fracture. We knew we couldn't extricate ourselves from the canyon due to the difficult terrain, so I pulled out the inReach, only to discover the batteries were dead. We next dialed 911 on my cell phone. The battery was low, having recorded our approach using the Gaia GPS application. To our surprise, a voice came on the other end, asking, "What's your emergency?" We explained our situation and indicated that we intended to rappel the route but would require assistance to evacuate.

We were starting the last rappel when we heard a helicopter approaching. A Pima County Sheriff's Department officer was lowered, and he hooked Steve up to the rescue cable. They flew him to an ambulance, which took him to a hospital in Tucson. I was left to return on my own and was able to get back to the truck without incident.

X-rays taken at the hospital showed that Steve's tibia was shattered into eight pieces. The fibula was, thankfully, not involved. This could have just as easily resulted in a fatality had he landed differently.

ANALYSIS

The duo was very experienced, having over 60 years of climbing between them. Sagin had climbed extensively in Mendoza Canyon, and this was his sixth time on Wily Javelina. Despite this, several factors contributed to an accident.

Cagle wrote to *ANAC*, "Failure to place protection and test holds were the biggest factors contributing directly to the accident. That said, I have routinely climbed easy ground without stopping to place pro, and it's not practical to test every hold on a route of that length.

"Several other failures that—but for luck—could have easily compounded the difficulty of our situation:

1. I failed to make certain the battery on the inReach was charged.
2. My cell phone battery wasn't fully charged when we left that morning. I had intended to charge it on the ride but didn't have a compatible cable.
3. On the approach, I didn't pay sufficient attention to our surroundings and let Steve lead the way while I chatted and followed blindly along. On the return, I depended heavily on the GPS track I had recorded on my phone. Had the phone failed, I am pretty sure I would've gotten lost and had to bivouac.

"As a result of this incident, I now strive when climbing or hiking to cultivate a mindset that assumes there will be an accident and to be fully prepared, both in skills and in resources." *(Source: Jerry Cagle.)*

Mt. Shasta (14,179 feet) from the north. In May, a climber became separated from his party at the summit and mistakenly descended onto the Whitney Glacier—seen here as the ice flowing below the col between the two highest peaks. *Frank Schulenburg | Wikimedia*

CALIFORNIA

SHASTA SEASON SUMMARY

The 2023 climbing season kicked off in early April, after a robust winter that brought well above average snowfall. With a nearly 200-inch base at 7,000 feet, skiers and climbers were eager to get on the mountain. Strong north wind events throughout the winter had left north-facing climbing routes with a thin snowpack and generally thinner snowpack above treeline.

In late June, the thin snowpack on the upper mountain began to melt and affect south-side climbing routes. Rockfall became the primary hazard for climbers, resulting in multiple accidents. In late July, climbing rangers began advising climbers not to climb Avalanche Gulch due to poor conditions. The remainder of the summer remained busy on east- and north-facing climbing routes. The Clear Creek Route on the mountain's east side remains a popular alternative for mid- to late-season climbing and for novice mountaineers; there is little to no rockfall due to its generally low angle. The route is not to be taken lightly, however, as we've had plenty of slips, trips, and falls on loose rock over the years, resulting in twisted and broken ankles. We've also had numerous exposure-related injuries from climbers becoming lost in poor weather. If you get off route, steep terrain does exist and slips/falls are not as friendly.

In 2023, we had ten SAR incidents on Mt. Shasta. This is about half of the average annual total of 20 incidents since 1992. The 2023 incidents consisted of one search, seven rescues, and two fatalities.

UNPLANNED BIVOUAC | Lost, Separated from Party
Mt. Shasta, Whitney Glacier

In near whiteout conditions on the afternoon of May 5, Adam Danielson (51) of Milwaukee, Wisconsin, separated from his party at the summit of Mt. Shasta at 2:45 p.m. Though he and his party had climbed Avalanche Gulch—a route that ascends the south side of the mountain—Danielson mistakenly descended to the north onto the Whitney Glacier. The remainder of his party, who were on skis, safely descended to their previous night's camp at Helen Lake. Danielson never arrived.

The weather during this period was winter-like, with rain, snow, wind, and very cold temperatures. Danielson didn't have reliable navigation tools, nor overnight equipment. He was equipped with a small pack, water, a bit of food, an ice axe, crampons, a helmet, snowshoes, and a cell phone. Danielson realized he was lost when he encountered glaciated terrain and large crevasses. He called 911 and began direct communication with the Siskiyou County Sheriff's Office and USFS climbing ranger Nick Meyers.

Cellular service was good at his location, and Danielson had an extra battery pack for his phone. Meyers told him that, regardless of any rescue plan, he was looking at an open overnight bivy. It would take rescuers four to six hours to get to his location by foot. Meyers suggested that Danielson descend if he could stay off the glacier, because a lower elevation would offer better protection from the weather. However, Danielson soon encountered a large crevasse and was afraid to move further. He was advised to shelter in place and that a rescue would launch in the morning.

Mt. Shasta climbing rangers ski onto the Whitney Glacier to rescue a stranded climber. **Nick Meyers | USFS**

At 5:30 a.m., continued poor weather prevented a helicopter rescue. Climbing rangers launched a ground rescue via the Northgate trailhead on snowmobile and skis. Siskiyou County SAR supported them with a snowcat and communications. Contact was made with Danielson at 12:30 p.m. at 11,600 feet on the Whitney Glacier. He was ambulatory, with a minor cold injury, and was escorted out to the Northgate trailhead by 4 p.m.; the sheriff's office then transported him several miles via snowcat to parked vehicles.

ANALYSIS

Danielson was humble and appreciative of the rescue efforts. Here are some take-home points:

- Check the weather before you climb and monitor conditions as you climb. Flexibility is one of the most important mountain skills. Be willing to change plans.
- Check your summit fever at the door. Don't summit late in the day.
- Carry navigation tools: map, compass, GPS, extra batteries or battery pack, etc. Know how to use them.

- Don't separate from your party. Make sure everyone is using the same mode of travel. In this case, Danielson was on foot and the rest of his party was on skis.
- Play the "what if" game: If things don't go as planned, what are you going to do? Often incidents don't involve injury but could involve environmental hazards like severe weather or an unplanned bivy. A small pad, bivy sack or tarp, and an extra down jacket can make a difference. *(Source: Mt. Shasta Climbing Rangers.)*

HYPOTHERMIA AND FROSTBITE | Summit Fever
Mt. Shasta, Avalanche Gulch
A 54-year-old, solo male climber attempted a car-to-car climb of Mt. Shasta, starting at midnight on Friday, April 21. He carried a small pack and no overnight equipment. Two local climbers encountered the man high on the mountain on Saturday, April 22. One of the climbers reported to the Mt. Shasta climbing rangers that:

"He was moving so slowly, sometimes on his hands and knees. I asked him if he needed anything. I told him that he didn't have to go up, but he certainly needed to go down. On my way back down from the summit, he was still only 50 or 60 feet higher. I told him I was a mountain guide and that he should come down the mountain with me. He asked if I thought he could make it to the summit in an hour. I told him it would take him at least four hours, and he'd have to descend in the dark. He absolutely refused to turn around."

At 4:15 a.m. on Sunday, April 23, Sam Kieckhefer, a guide, was ascending with a client…"when he encountered the distressed climber. He contacted the Siskiyou County Sheriff's Office and USFS ranger Nick Meyers. The climber had been descending and was at 9,200 feet. He was cold, disoriented, and mildly combative. He was wearing no shoes, socks, or gloves. His equipment was spread out on the slope. In an incident report submitted to the rangers, Kieckhefer wrote:

"The climber was barefoot, feet white and bloody, toenails missing or lifted off the bed. He was holding his phone. Initially I asked him how I could help, and he said he didn't need help. He believed he was at home and was looking for blankets because he was cold. He was insistent that he did not want us to help him and that he was fine. I would characterize the climber as severely disoriented and borderline combative. My biggest concern was him trying to move because the snow was extremely firm and he was positioned on a slope [creating a fall hazard].

"After notifying 911 of the nature of the emergency and our location, they asked we stay with the climber. I received a call from the Siskiyou County sheriff… to tell me they were aware of our situation and were working on it.

"During/after these two calls, we gathered [the climber's] boots, socks, gloves, and pack. He was more willing to accept help at this time. We immediately dug a flat platform for him to sit, helped him put his socks and boots on, got him in all of his layers and a few of ours. We also put him in an emergency bivy and gave him water and some food. In this process, we noticed he had a Jetboil and began boiling. After warming a bit, the climber's awareness improved dramatically, and after about an hour he reported that he was feeling better but could not feel his feet."

At 7:49 a.m. the distressed climber was helicoptered to safety and treatment.

It almost goes without saying that pushing too hard on a mountain can be hazardous to the climber and to those who provide assistance.

Kieckhefer reported that the climber had reached the top of the Red Banks (13,110 feet) at 2 p.m. and reported feeling quite exhausted. Because of the proximity to the summit, he decided to rest, eat, and drink and then push on. He began climbing Misery Hill (13,840 feet) at 3 p.m., and we estimate he summited around 5 p.m. From there, details are unclear, but he obviously became disoriented and hypothermic as he was descending. He was out through the night with no sleeping bag or tent. *(Sources: Mt. Shasta Climbing Rangers and Sam Kieckhefer.)*

ERRONEOUS REPORTING
Mt. Shasta, Clear Creek Route
On June 16, Siskiyou County was notified of a missing climber on the Clear Creek Route of Mt. Shasta. The climber had been overdue for 30 hours, and loved ones had lost communication and called 911. Mt. Shasta climbing rangers mobilized to the trailhead to begin search efforts on snowmobiles and skis. A California Highway Patrol (CHP) helicopter was launched and was quickly able to spot a climber descending the mountain at around 10,000 feet. CHP made visual and verbal contact with the climber and positively identified him as the missing climber. The climber indicated that he did not want help. CHP and the climbing rangers stood down.

On June 18, two days later, climbing rangers were again notified by the Siskiyou County Sheriff's Office that the same climber was still missing and had once again stopped communication with family. Rangers mobilized to begin a search. Two climbing rangers launched from the Clear Creek trailhead on snowmobiles, while two other rangers prepared for a CHP helicopter insertion onto the upper mountain. Just then, the climber, who had emerged onto a road, was located a quarter mile from the trailhead. The climber was in good condition, and all staff returned home.

While 911 undeniably saves lives every year, it comes with disadvantages, including use of the service for non-emergency situations and, in this case, the issue of erroneous reporting. Even the best-intended false report can squander valuable rescuer time and resources and burden an overtaxed system. It might even impede a real emergency response. These 911 calls were placed by family members, never by the climber himself. In both instances, the climber was surprised to see SAR members and was not in need of help. It is important that the climber keep their loved ones or emergency contact updated as necessary. The climber had been on the mountain for five or six days on a route that normally takes one to two days. *(Source: Mt. Shasta Climbing Rangers.)*

FATAL FALL DURING DESCENT
Yosemite National Park, Tenaya Peak
On July 21, Yosemite dispatch received an emergency alert from Tenaya Lake's East Beach. Initial reports indicated that a climber in his 50s had taken a tumbling fall on Tenaya Peak and was not breathing. The first ranger arrived at the Tenaya East

Beach parking lot at 11:58 a.m. and made contact with the injured climber's partner. The injured climber was reported to be both apneic (not breathing) and pulseless.

The ranger and the injured climber's partner began hiking toward the accident location. When the ranger arrived on scene, they assessed the patient and pronounced the climber's death at 12:44 p.m.

The ranger also documented all details of the scene. Another Yosemite ranger conducted a field interview with the climbing partner, during which it was revealed that the fatal fall occurred while descending from Tenaya Peak. The terrain consisted of low brush, loose sand, gravel, and boulders. The area included sections of 3rd- and 4th-class terrain, as well as wet and slippery sections due to water and snow.

The climbing partner had witnessed an earlier fall, when the climber slid several feet after loose dirt dislodged beneath him. Despite the partner's effort to encourage the climber to move toward a more stable area, their descent path continued in this terrain. The deceased climber ultimately slid again and came to rest 200 to 250 feet below his climbing partner. After the fall, the climbing partner ran to Tenaya Lake to seek help, due to limited cell service on the mountain.

A ranger and a SAR technician remained with the deceased climber while the climbing partner and another ranger hiked back to Tenaya Lake. At 6:26 p.m., the park helicopter airlifted the climber's remains via long-line for transport to the Crane Flat Helibase.

ANALYSIS

- **Plan Your Descent:** Before ascending any route, climbers should also plan the descent. The preferred descent route, the location of rappel anchors, and the ideal path back to the trailhead should all be identified.
- **Stay Within Your Ability:** Choose descents that match the skill level and experience of each climber on a team. If uncertain about a particular descent, seek guidance and information from experienced climbers.
- **Weather Awareness:** Climbers should monitor changing weather conditions, which can impact a descent, especially on exposed routes. Plans should always include emergency shelter and retreat options.
- **Rescue and Communications:** Teams should carry some means of reliable communication in the event of an emergency, such as a charged cell phone or a satellite communication device. Be aware of limited cell service in certain areas. *(Source: Yosemite National Park Climbing Rangers.)*

FATAL ROCKFALL
Yosemite National Park, Leaning Tower

On the afternoon of June 19, two teams were descending from Leaning Tower. The descent, which is known to be challenging, was the site of a devastating accident and a male climber in his 40s lost his life.

While the lower team was trying to find an anchor, the climbing team above them began rappelling atop the same gully. One of the climbers in the second team was rappelling when they dislodged a four-foot by two-foot by six-inch rock. The climbers yelled, "Rock" as the block fell down the descent gully and began dislodging additional rocks and debris along the way.

The fixed haul line on which one member of the lower team was descending was severed by the rockfall approximately 50 feet below the anchor. The climber on the cut rope fell approximately 300 feet and died on impact. Both teams called 911 to report the accident as they continued descending to render aid.

ANALYSIS

This unfortunate incident highlights the risks inherent to descending, especially when traveling or rappelling through loose rock. The Leaning Tower rappels follow a notoriously loose gully and are especially dangerous. Climbers often focus heavily on managing risks during the ascent but should also dedicate the same meticulous attention to safety during descent.

The Yosemite climbing rangers provided the following reminders for readers:

- **Rappel Safety.** Climbers should exercise extreme caution during rappel descents, particularly in areas with loose rock. It's imperative to be mindful of the potential for rockfall and to take precautions to minimize risk.
- **Helmet Use.** Wearing a climbing helmet is of utmost importance, not only during the ascent but also during descent. A helmet can provide protection against falling debris and significantly reduce the risk of head injuries.
- **Communication and Spacing.** Climbing teams should communicate with other teams during rappel descents. Maintaining ample spacing between teams can mitigate accidental rockfall incidents. Though it is not always convenient, consider spending additional time before beginning a descent to allow adequate spacing between parties.
- **Rope Management.** Proper rope management is essential to avoid entanglements and ensure ropes do not dislodge debris during rope retrieval. Consider rappelling with ropes connected to a climbing harness; the "saddlebag" technique minimizes the risk of rope tails dislodging debris.
- **Route Assessment.** Prior to descent, climbers should assess the route for potential hazards, such as loose rock and other dangers. Research online updates and information. This evaluation can inform decision-making and tactics.
- **Community Impact.** This incident is a somber reminder of the collective responsibility within our community to prioritize safety, communicate openly, and adhere to best practices. Climbers should remain vigilant, respect risks, and continually work to minimize accident potential. The loss of a climber's life underscores the need for a shared commitment to safety and preparedness. As a reminder, the climbing community has resources, like the Climbing Grief Fund, for those experiencing hardship secondary to a climbing-related accident. *(Source: Yosemite National Park Climbing Rangers.)*

LEADER FALL | Inadequate Protection
Yosemite National Park, Half Dome

On July 7, two male climbers in their 30s began a proposed three-day climb of Half Dome's Regular Northwest Face (VI 5.9 C1). Their plan was to fix the initial three pitches on the first day, climb to the Big Sandy ledge the following day, and then summit on the third day.

The climb was unfolding well until they arrived at pitch eight, the start of a long

The Regular Northwest Face of Half Dome saw a serious leader fall on July 7 (yellow circle) when a cam pulled out. *Tuxyso | Wikimedia*

traverse up and right. The leader encountered difficult route-finding on chossy but easy terrain. He began to wonder if he was off route, as rock quality began to deteriorate and signs of wear from past climbers became less obvious. Nevertheless, the leader continued climbing in hopes of getting back on route.

Due to the wandering nature of the pitch, this climber decided to remove a previous piece of protection to prevent rope drag. The climber placed a 0.3 cam in what appeared to be solid rock, planning to lower off this new piece in order to clean the previous cam. When the climber weighted the 0.3 cam, the surrounding rock broke, causing a 40-to-50-foot tumbling fall. Several other pieces of protection pulled, contributing to the substantial fall.

After being caught by the rope, the fallen climber realized he had sustained several injuries, causing an unusable foot and back mobility issues. He had several abrasions. This climber also realized that the gear loop containing his anchor-building materials and belay device had been torn off. A short time later, the team called NPS personnel for rescue assistance and began a tedious rappel toward the ground.

The team was able to self-rescue to the ground. Fortunately, another team had fixed the first three pitches, making for easier rappels. At the base, the climbers were met by two NPS climbing rangers on a Half Dome patrol. The rangers assessed the injured climber and decided it was appropriate to extract the patient via helicopter. Two additional NPS rescuers were inserted into the scene with a litter. The patient was packaged and extracted via short-haul. The patient's partner spent the night at the base of the route and hiked out the following day.

ANALYSIS

The Yosemite climbing rangers remind readers of the following safety measures pertinent to this incident:

- **Do not underestimate easy terrain.** It is common for experienced and inexperienced climbers to get injured or killed in easy terrain. Letting one's guard down increases the likelihood of an accident. Regardless of the relative difficulty, continue to be mindful and situationally aware.

  The climber who fell, later said: "If this fall had happened on steeper or harder terrain, the consequences would have been minor. The terrain that I often consider easy or safe is actually the most unstable and consequential."

- **Contact rescue personnel ASAP.** Organizing a rescue is often time-consuming. The rangers recommend contacting rescue personnel as soon as it is evident that outside resources are needed. In this instance, the injured climber's partner contacted YOSAR first thing, even though rescue was not immediately needed. This allowed SAR additional time to plan and launch the helicopter prior to sunset, thus retrieving the injured climber on the same day.

- **Maximize route familiarization.** Climbers should carefully study climbing and descent routes ahead of time. This information can be gleaned from topos and by seeking beta from experienced climbers. These efforts can enhance route-finding and overall safety by helping to prevent diversions onto unstable terrain. *(Source: Yosemite National Park Climbing Rangers.)*

ROCKFALL | Large Flake Detached on Follower
Yosemite National Park, Yosemite Falls Wall

On July 7, two male climbers in their 20s were attempting Via Aqua on Yosemite Falls Wall. Via Aqua is an adventurous and lesser-known classic four-pitch 5.8 climb. The climbers were progressing up the wall when disaster struck. While one climber was following an angled flake feature on pitch three, a sizable section of the flake detached from the wall, impacted the climber's left shoulder, and tore off a portion of his left ear. Luckily, the rope was not severed by the flake and caught his fall.

After his fall, and despite his injuries, the climber was able to climb 15 to 20 feet up to his partner's stance. The team called 911 for a rescue. They noted that the injured climber was "covered in blood" that originated from a five-inch-long laceration on his shoulder. The tissue was exposed down to the muscle, and the bleeding from this wound was life-threatening.

Recognizing the urgency of rescue, NPS personnel conducted a timely short-haul operation from the climbers' small belay ledge. Once on the ground, the climber was transferred to an ambulance for transport to definitive care at a local hospital.

ANALYSIS

This incident highlights a few considerations for climbers in Yosemite:

- **Impacts of Freeze-Thaw Cycles.** The historic snowfall during the winter of 2022-2023, followed by spring freeze/thaw cycles, caused much of the granite in the park to expand and contract. This phenomenon caused rock to detach from various walls and pose risks to climbers. Climbers are advised to consider previous environmental conditions and those impacts on their chosen routes.
- **Medical Training and Equipment.** Carrying first aid on a climb is highly recommended. Useful items include medical tape, gauze, pain medication, and material to create a sling and swath. These items can be improvised out of clothing and climbing equipment. This injured climber was remarkably lucky. If the falling flake had cut the interior of his arm (brachial artery), it could have been lethal. Knowing how to apply direct pressure to a bleed and create a tourniquet could be a lifesaver. Having medical tools and training should be expected of all climbing partners.
- **Self-Rescue Proficiency.** The incident highlighted the importance of maintaining self-rescue skills. Baseline skills include safe ascent and descent of ropes, escape from belay systems, and improvising emergency solutions. While

Via Aqua (4 pitches, 5.8) is moderate climb characterized by its wandering route-finding, subpar rock quality, and stunning views. This unique route (yellow line) crosses a huge, massively exposed ledge system two-thirds of the way up the 1,500-foot-tall Yosemite Falls Wall. On July 7, this route was the scene of a serious though non-fatal rockfall incident. *Alex Demas | USGS*

SAR can provide assistance, the climbing team itself is best able to address urgent situations. Self-rescue skills should be a priority for climbers of all levels. *(Source: Yosemite National Park Climbing Rangers.)*

FATAL UNROPED FALL
Yosemite National Park, El Capitan

On October 2, a 55-year-old male was reported missing by his son. The missing climber had failed to return from a solo attempt on the West Gully of El Capitan. Members of Yosemite Search and Rescue (YOSAR) were deployed, and after a few hours of searching, the body of the missing climber was located near the base of the gully. He had sustained fatal injuries.

The West Gully is a historic route dating back to 1905. Of note, one of the first ascensionists also took a fatal fall. The route has an easy technical grade (5.5) but is notorious for loose rock and difficult route-finding. Many climbers and hikers underestimate the complexities of this climb when seeking a route to the summit of El Capitan.

The terrain in the West Gully is steep, rocky, and vegetated. Ultimately, the team decided that lowering systems and guiding lines would expose personnel to the least hazard. Multiple hours were required for rigging and recovery.

The cause of death was cranial trauma secondary to either a fall or being struck by a falling rock. The exact sequence of events leading to the fall remains unclear, but it is likely that the climber slipped, broke a hold, or fell while climbing off route.

Contributing factors in this incident included:

- **Lack of Protective Equipment.** The climber was not wearing a helmet, which could have mitigated or prevented the fatal head injury.
- **Terrain Challenges.** El Capitan's West Gully has 4th- and 5th-class terrain. This terrain may have exceeded the skill level of the deceased climber.
- **Solo Climbing.** Embarking on any climb without a partner reduces one's ability to receive immediate aid or outside assistance in the event of an accident.
- **Route Information.** Despite its being a technical climbing route, West Gully route information is shared on numerous hiking apps and websites. When researching a technical climb, it is best to gather information from fellow climbers and climbing-specific resources. *(Source: Yosemite National Park Climbing Rangers.)*

IMPALEMENT ON CAM
Yosemite National Park, El Capitan

On October 20, Gabe Hayden, Dylan Miller, and I were climbing the Freeblast (10 pitches, 5.11) on our way to attempt The Shield (VI 5.8 A3) on El Cap. My partners both had experience on the Freeblast, and they led us through the harder pitches, pulling on gear when necessary to keep up our pace and navigate around other parties.

I got the last, easier block. Having spent the preceding months on a commercial fishing boat, I had very little climbing fitness. Nonetheless, there is only one opportunity to onsight, and I assumed I could manage the pitches. Pulling into the Half Dollar flake (5.10), I made a rookie mistake and placed a cam in the only available finger lock. I decided I could work around it and, spying some faint chalk on the arête, I thought I'd outsmart the section with a few moves of face climbing. I did not find the jugs I had hoped for, and soon I was overcommitted.

Cole Taylor climbing into trouble on the Half Dollar Pitch of Freeblast. He fell shortly after this photo was taken, impacting a slab (out of sight). On impact, his leg became impaled on a Camalot's lobe. *Dylan Miller*

I groped upward, hoping to climb my way out of the pickle, but soon fell. Because I had ventured onto the arête, I fell from an awkward, stemmed-out position and smacked hard onto the slab. I then slid several feet until the rope caught. Ouch!

I shook it off and finished the pitch, but I had a lingering charley horse. I carried on through the last pitch, but by the time I reached Mammoth Terrace, I noticed blood on my leg and knew the injury was worse than a charley horse. It seemed I'd fallen onto one of my cams and it had cut my leg. When my partners arrived, I took off my harness, pulled down my pants, and rolled away so they could see the wound. Dylan was impressed by the very deep incision. He said, "I can't even see the bottom, it just goes black in there." Gabe took one look and said, "Yup, we're going down."

Still mobile, I took the portaledge and headed down the fixed ropes, leaving Dylan and Gabe to dump all of our precious water and wrestle the pigs down. I borrowed Dylan's car and drove myself to the Valley medical clinic at about 3 p.m. There, I learned they close at 1 p.m. on Fridays and stay closed all weekend. I was lucky to find a nurse on-site, and he gave me some saline and gauze and sent me on my way.

Back at El Cap Meadow, my partners helped me irrigate and bandage the wound, then drove me to urgent care in Oakhurst, where I got seven stitches. The next afternoon, I thumbed through the rack, wondering which cam had punctured me. The hole in my leg had been large enough for a yellow Totem, but Gabe and Dylan were adamant that it had to have been the number 3 Camalot. Closer inspection revealed blood and a gob of flesh stuck to one of the lobes.

ANALYSIS

This was not a serious injury, but it was seriously novel. I would put it on a list of things you would rather not know: You can be impaled by the cams hanging on your harness. Is there a valuable takeaway from this incident? I think Gabe said it best: "Don't deck onto the slab." *(Source: Cole Taylor.)*

PINNED UNDER BOULDER
Inyo National Forest, Lamarck Col

Around 12:40 p.m. on September 28, Larsen Tormey (28) was pinned under a large boulder while hiking out after an attempt on the Evolution Traverse (IV 5.9). His climbing partner, Jacob Ireland (35), was able to free him after several hours, prior to the arrival of SAR.

Ireland wrote to *ANAC*:

The accident took place five miles from the trailhead. Lars was hiking ahead of me. I was at the top of Lamarck Col when I heard someone yelling. I figured this was Lars, but I couldn't spot him. As I headed toward the sound the cries grew louder, and I knew that an accident had occurred. When I was directly above his voice, I could hear clearly, "I'm stuck! There's a rock on me! Please help!"

I hit the SOS button on my Garmin inReach and started down the broken 4th-class terrain. When I made it to Lars, he explained that, because he carried no traction devices nor ice axe, he had been downclimbing through a small tunnel or cave in the rock to avoid a steep section of hard-packed snow. A boulder the size of a city trash can he had been using as a hold came free. The rock was angled and sharp and plugged the slot so his leg was pinned just below his groin.

The boulder was in the way, so I couldn't see his injuries and had to rely on what he told me. From what I could tell, one leg was pinned near his groin. It's hard to recall, but the rock was maybe three feet by three feet and one foot wide.

There was no blood, but Lars believed he was bleeding internally and could not feel his leg. He was lying partly on the ice and was cold and shaking. I did my best to drape a puffy over him. I tried to move the boulder, but this only made him scream. The back of the rock was the obvious place to try moving it, but I quickly realized it wasn't going to move by hand. I told Lars I was going to try the climbing

Larsen Tormey, three hours after being pinned by a large boulder near Lamarck Col. This photo was taken shortly before his partner managed to pull the boulder off. *Jacob Ireland*

rope and gear we had brought.

He pleaded with me to just try by hand again, and I did my best to assure him that the rope would be better. I frantically unpacked my gear. I jammed a cam into a crack above us, wrapped the rope around the front of the boulder, and set up a hauling system with my harness and two Micro Traxions.

The next hour was a blur. We tried multiple configurations of the rope and hauling methods. Nothing worked beyond a small amount of movement. One method from the side caused Lars to cry out, "Stop! You're making it worse!" Between all my attempts, poor Lars begged me to keep trying. Every now and then we made eye contact, and I could see his horror and pain. I'd exhausted myself and started needing longer breaks between tries. My hand was bleeding, so I wrapped it with climbing tape. I had to cut the rope multiple times to quickly fix jams when I'd reset a system. Everything was failing.

I realized my phone had been getting messages. I had cell service and called 911 and relayed information. Lars was screaming at me to keep trying. He didn't believe help was going to come fast enough. Part of me believed him, so I did my best to talk on the phone and work on the boulder at the same time. Someone from the Inyo SAR team called back and I sent them photos and exact coordinates. They assured me they were on the way.

It had been almost three hours since the boulder fell on Lars, and I was beginning to lose hope. Every failed attempt was devastating. I felt weak and my hips were raw and bruised from the harness. Then, in one adrenaline-fueled attempt, I clipped my harness directly to the rope around the boulder via a sling and pulled to the side. The boulder started to move. My foot gained a bit of new leverage and the boulder moved more. Lars began yelling that he was able to move. "Keep going!" I found a hold in the back of the wall and pulled as hard as I could, screaming from the adrenaline and pain in my waist.

Lars slipped down and behind the boulder to a larger ledge below. He was free and I was ecstatic. I used the rope to swing down to him. He was shaking, cold, and couldn't feel his leg. I got him flat and bundled up with both sleeping bags and an air mattress under his body. He was in and out of consciousness, but his breathing remained stable. I checked his wound, and to my astonishment it didn't look worse than a large bruise. Of course, I had no idea what was happening internally.

An hour and a half later, a helicopter appeared and I felt massive relief. The U.S. Army had been flying training missions in the area, and the SAR team was able to use their Chinook helicopter to reach us. They landed at the bottom of the snowfield. An hour later Lars was in the chopper heading for Fresno. He suffered abrasions, major impact trauma, nerve damage, and internal bleeding. He still has trouble making large upward steps, but he is out hiking, biking, and getting back to normal.

ANALYSIS

I think the main factors in this accident were:

1. **Lack of gear for snow travel:** We should have had Microspikes or crampons and an ice axe. With those items, we would have directly descended the snow in Lamarck Col and avoided the loose rock.

2. **Getting separated:** With our technical objective behind us, we became complacent. Had we stuck together, we might have chosen a different way or at least been able to help each other sooner. Lars spent almost an hour under the boulder before I found him. Had he been unconscious, I might have passed by and not realized he was missing until hours later.

3. **More knowledge of hauling systems and pulleys:** I tried a number of techniques with the climbing gear on hand. A few of these systems moved the boulder, but not enough to free Lars. If I had more knowledge, I could have rigged something to free him faster. *(Source: Jacob Ireland.)*

TOP-ROPE SOLO FALL | Device Jammed by Sling
Sequoia National Park, Angel Wings

On October 8, Whitney Clark was ascending a fixed rope at the start of Valkyrie (17 pitches, 5.11+) when her single ascension device was jammed by a sling. She fell 30 feet to the ground.

Clark wrote to *ANAC*:

"We woke at around 6 a.m. and made our way to the fixed line from the day before. The days were short, and we had many pitches to do. My partner, Luka Krajnc, went first, using a Grigri to jug and then transitioning to climbing. About 40 feet up, he clove-hitched the rope to a bolt. I then started jugging with a single Micro Traxion. Thirty feet up, I leaned back on the rope. My body weight wasn't supported because the sling around my neck [part of the top-rope solo setup] got sucked into the device and caught in the teeth of the Traxion. The rope was sliding against the sling. I hadn't tied a backup knot."

Whitney Clark's progress-capture device failed when the as-yet-unused retention sling got stuck in the device as she was ascending. It is common practice to use a sling and an elastic connection to hold the progress-capture device upright as one climbs along a fixed rope. *Luka Krajnc*

Clark attempted to wrap the rope around her leg. But her rope was new, thin, and slippery. She wrote, "I grabbed the rope and slowly started sliding down. Eventually the rope burn was too painful and I let go. I hit the ground, landed on my feet, and fell backward. I struck my lower back and then my head. I was wearing a helmet. Because the ground was angled, some of the force was dissipated, though I landed six inches from a large rock spike.

"I never lost consciousness, but was in a bit of shock. Luka rappelled down and did a spinal exam. He got me comfortable, and I sat there for a while. I had pain in my back and my left ankle. I used my inReach to call for a rescue while Luka retrieved our stuff. I started crawling and butt-scooting to where a heli could reach me. I would have loved to have self-rescued, but it's a 16-mile hike out. It took about 2.5 hours of crawling to make it to a flat place. Four hours later, a helicopter airlifted me to the Visalia Level III trauma center."

ANALYSIS

Solo top-roping is integral to many forms of modern climbing. It allows a climber to self-belay when no partner is available, for a team to work on individual sections of a route without the need for a belayer, or for two climbers to move simultaneously, as in this situation. The errors Clark made were using only one device to safeguard her progress and not tying a backup knot.

"I was jugging by pulling on the rope, syncing up the slack, and sitting back," Clark said. "The route was meandering, and the fixed line didn't allow me to readily climb, so I decided to jug straight up the initial blank slab. The sling around my neck was going to hold the Traxion upright [allowing the rope to feed freely] once I started climbing. I haven't done any top-rope soloing since the accident. I probably will at some point, but I will definitely use two devices. This was the first time I only used a single progress-capture device." *(Source: Whitney Clark.)*

FALL ON ROCK | Communication Error, Taken Off Belay
Malibu, Point Dume State Park

On October 9, we decided to go to the beachside cliff at Point Dume because my partner (female, 24) had never been and I, Ben Nutter (26), used to love to rope-solo there. We walked to the top, set up the anchors for the top-rope, and then rappelled down. The anchor was a quad sling on two bolts. I went first. I believe the route was Right Center (5.7). I climbed to the top and did what I normally do when I get to the top of a climb. I leaned back into my harness and onto the rope, then I fell all the way to the bottom.

I landed on the sand near my partner. Someone nearby had seen the fall and called 911. A lifeguard came over and stayed until a helicopter came to take me to an intensive-care unit. I am alive and can walk, but I suffered a traumatic brain injury.

ANALYSIS

My partner had detached her Grigri, thinking I would move the anchor after I had finished climbing. She probably thought I would belay her from the top. The issue was that she didn't communicate either of these thoughts with me, and I didn't call out any relevant commands when I got to the anchor.

Point Dume State Park is a popular seaside area with short top-ropes. Last year, Right Center (5.7) was the site of a serious lowering accident. *Cecily Breeding | Wikimedia*

Be on the same page with your partner about the climbing plan. Communicate and know what's going on with your partner to make sure they're safe. Do not assume anything! *(Source: Ben Nutter.)*

*Editor's Note: This type of accident happens all too frequently, to novices and veteran climbers alike (see ANAC 2012). As Ben suggests, there is no such thing as too much relevant communication before a climb and when a climber reaches the anchor. However, be clear with your words and intentions. Vague terms like "Okay?" and "Okay!" are frequently used and can mean any number of things.

BOULDERING FALL | Insufficient Pads
Joshua Tree National Park, Hidden Valley Area

On November 9, Gibson McGee (19) was bouldering on White Rastafarian, a V2 highball (some say V3) that has been the scene of many accidents. He fell from near the top and struck the ground, shattering his L1 vertebra (the highest bone in the lower back).

Though Mountain Project describes White Rastafarian as "one of JTree's finest problems," the climb is 25 feet tall—more like a short route instead of a boulder problem. After the midpoint crux, the climber is faced with a tricky mantel top-out.

McGee wrote to *ANAC*, "I was heading to Joshua Tree for the weekend, and I was planning on meeting a group who were coming in the following morning. After setting up camp, I went to go climb the nearby White Rastafarian. I had previously attempted it but fell at the crux [15 feet off ground]. I was fine with no injuries." McGee laid out three crash pads, set up a video camera to record himself, and started up the route.

"I got to the top of the route [about 25 feet off ground] and was too pumped to do the 'easy' mantel onto the top of the rock. I looked down and decided I could drop safely. I dropped, but when I hit the ground, I ended up shattering my L1 vertebra. I then crawled to the nearby Hidden Valley Campground, where I got help and was transported by ambulance to the Hi Desert Medical Center."

As of November 2023, McGee was recovering. He wrote, "While I am eager to be able to climb again, healing physically and mentally will take quite some time. I was very fortunate, looking back on the possible injuries I could've sustained."

ANALYSIS

Bouldering is inherently dangerous, and highball problems particularly so. On Reddit, "un poco lobo" posted, "Was chatting with a park ranger who said they see more accidents on WR [White Rastafarian] than pretty much all other routes/problems combined."

McGee had been climbing outdoors consistently for the year prior. He wrote, "I saw White Rastafarian the first week I started climbing. It has always been a dream for me to do it." His pad placements were correct, and he landed cleanly—no part of his body struck exposed ground. While multiple pads are a great idea, an evenly distributed second layer of pads might have saved McGee from a trip to the hospital. Covering gaps between pads with a thin "slider" pad also would have provided additional safety. McGee mentioned, "I should've brought a buddy and stacked bouldering pads."

For highballs, spotters need to be careful (and may even be extraneous), as the impact forces of a falling climber can be equally harmful to the spotter. While spotting highballs is more art than science, the general rule is to ensure that the falling climber stays on the pad after impact. (Guaranteeing that the climber impacts the pad itself is part of good pad placement.) A spotter should also protect the climber's head and neck from impacting bare ground or surrounding obstacles. Another good rule to follow is to never fall above the 20-foot mark. Be open to using a top-rope to practice the problem. The great John Gill himself was a big exponent of top-roping.

Finally, Joshua Tree has a well-earned reputation for tricky climbing with a long learning curve. Different climbing areas have special characteristics that a grade does not necessarily convey. It's a good idea to be conservative as you learn the peculiarities of an area. Said McGee, "I have bouldered in Joshua Tree four or five times. The grading is much, much harder than what you might think. I let the number [V2] get in my head rather than trusting the true difficulty of J-Tree grades." *(Sources: Gibson McGee, Mountain Project, Climbing magazine, Reddit, and the Editors.)*

FREE SOLOIST RESCUE
El Cajon Mountain, The Wedge

On February 12, Brent Donovan and Chase Morgan were hiking to El Cajon Mountain (ECM), east of San Diego, for a day of rock climbing. They were interrupted when they saw a free soloist stranded on the first pitch of Leonids. Free soloist Nathaniel Takatsuno fell from Leonids (3 pitches, 5.9) several months prior, on December 4, 2022.

Morgan wrote to *ANAC*:

Brent and I started up the trail around 7 a.m. ECM has an ass-kicker of an approach that gains nearly 2,000 feet of elevation in less than two miles. About 30 minutes into the approach, we were close enough to the wall to make out a person hanging out below one of the crux moves of Leonids. Our initial impression was that a person was hanging out five bolts up, trying to get it together to pull the slippery layback move. We both joked about having been in that spot more than once. Despite being an "easy" route, that move never feels secure.

Farther up the trail, the person came back into view, and he was still in the same spot. We figured it was a newer climber struggling on the move. When we got to the base around 8:30 or 8:45 a.m., the climber had been stuck for at least one hour. By the time we realized he was unroped, he was yelling for help.

He told us he couldn't downclimb the 45 feet below because he was "definitely going to fall" if he tried. He also said he thought if he had soloed the route, he could downclimb to the right (the actual 4th-class downclimb is to the left—to the right involves pitches up to 5.10). I told him to sit tight. He mentioned having a harness and quickdraws in his bag at the base of the cliff, but no rope. It was unclear what his plan was with the gear, but it made the rescue easier. I would put him at college age, late teens to early 20s.

I grabbed his harness and some of his draws and led up to him on my rope. I clipped a draw to the bolt that was shoulder level with him (the fifth bolt, about 45 feet up) and tied a quad-length sling around his waist. I secured the sling to my belay loop with a locker, while he slipped on his harness. The stance was uncomfortable (his calves were probably on fire at this point), but good enough for him to go hands-free. After he was harnessed up, I attached his belay loop to my belay loop with a sling and a locker. I had Brent take tight on the rope and lower us both. I then went up and back-cleaned all the draws but the top one. (A friend climbed the route and returned that draw later in the day.) The whole rescue took less than 15 minutes.

El Cajon Mountain is a bad place to solo. Few routes have a walk-off, and the climbing is often thin face on brittle holds. We tried to get as much of the story as we could from him, but he was reluctant to share details and seemed quite embarrassed. He took off down the trail almost immediately after we got him to the ground, even though we told him that if he waited 15 minutes we could get his quickdraws for him. We learned he had never climbed at ECM before (possibly never outside a gym) and was completely unaware that a 22-year-old [Takatsuno] had died on the same route only two months prior.

His harness and shoes were almost brand-new, and his quickdraws still had price tags on them. There seemed to be complete lack of awareness of the limitations of his ability and of the terrain he was entering. I can only speculate why he chose to solo. He looked to be in pretty good shape, so my guess is that he climbs pretty hard in the gym and felt that 5.9 would be easy. He expressed that it was a stupid decision and that he would never do it again.

While I hate to see people get themselves into these situations, I would hate even more to find his mangled body on the ground. I'm glad he waited for people to show up instead of getting himself hurt—although he probably would have downclimbed just fine. San Diego has seen a disproportionate share of free solo fatalities recently, between the two ECM deaths* and Mike Spitz's fall off Illusion Dweller in Joshua Tree (*see ANAC 2023*). I'll take an embarrassed soloist over a fatality any day. *(Sources: Chase Morgan and Brent Donovan.)*

*Editor's Note: On July 31, 2023, Adam Shmidt (34) died while free soloing Sleeping Giant (1,000 feet, 5.10a), also on El Cajon Mountain.

The stranded free soloist above was rescued shortly after this photo was taken. One of the rescuers was Chase Morgan. He wrote to ANAC, "The soloist was standing on a sloping foot ledge, just below the slippery crux, about 45 feet off the ground. He'd been there for at least an hour— more likely two." **Brent Donovan**

An Army Black Hawk helicopter lifts the severely injured Becca Steinbrecher out of the Black Canyon on September 11, 2023. *Vic Zeilman*

COLORADO

LEDGE FALL | Foothold Broke, Protection Pulled Out
Black Canyon of the Gunnison, Long Draw

Around 7:30 a.m. on September 11, Becca Steinbrecher (30) took a serious leader fall on Great White Wall (1,300 feet, 5.10d), below the North Rim in the Black Canyon. She fell at the beginning of pitch four on a relatively easy pegmatite ramp (5.8), 300 feet above the ground. As she started up from the belay on a sloping, broken terrace, protection was sparse. She ventured off route in search of gear. After placing a number 2 Metolius TCU, she made her way back to the pegmatite ramp. As she attempted a mantel, a foothold broke. The rock around the TCU fractured, and the protection pulled. Becca fell 30 feet to the terraced ledge and was knocked unconscious.

Her climbing partner, Skyeler Congdon (40), did not move her because he was concerned about a spinal cord injury. "There's like no good answer for that situation," he later said in an interview with the *Grand Junction Daily Sentinel*. After a half an hour, he decided to secure Becca to an anchor, rappel the route, and retrace the team's approach up the Long Draw (gully). From there, he planned to seek help at the North Rim ranger station. The station was about an hour's hike from the base of the route.

When Congdon arrived, there was no one at the ranger station. He then drove his car to get cell reception up the road. He called 911 and eventually his report was forwarded to Black Canyon ranger Ryan Rees, who began preparations for the rescue and passed Incident Command to district ranger Ryan Thrush. They rounded up a SAR team that eventually numbered 28 personnel and secured a helicopter from the Army National Guard High-Altitude Aviation Training Site (HAATS) at Eagle, Colorado.

By 1:20 p.m., the SAR team had assembled at the ranger station. Becca had been on the pitch-four ledge for over five hours. It was unknown if she was still alive.

Vic Zeilman, a former NPS climbing ranger and Black Canyon guidebook author, was a SAR volunteer on that day. He wrote to *ANAC*: "I would describe the rescue as being multifaceted, time sensitive, and complex, with a lot of unknowns right out of the gate. For that reason, we had a Plan A and Plan B happening simultaneously. Plan A was to utilize aviation resources if it was possible to either short-haul or hoist Becca. Plan B was to lower an attendant from the rim to near the base of the Great White Wall so that Becca could be raised back to the rim."

Both plans required that SAR personnel descend into the canyon, climb to Becca, and then lower her to the base of the climb. From there, she could be lowered down-gully to a more open area near the bottom of the canyon and airlifted (Plan A) or delivered to a team to be raised 1,300 feet to the rim (Plan B).

A climbing team including Zeilman, and led by NPS ranger Philippe Wheelock, departed at 1:45 p.m. They descended Long Draw and climbed to Becca. They radioed climbing NPS ranger Tom Schaefer—who was manning operations on the canyon rim—that Becca was unconscious but alive.

It was 4 p.m., and it would take over an hour for the HAATS helicopter to arrive. With sunset at 7:30 p.m., there was an ever-narrowing window for aerial extraction, as HAATS would not fly into the canyon in the dark. In the meantime, Schaefer had organized Plan B. This contingency required two rescue teams—one to rig the immense litter raise and another team to help transport the patient to the raise location.

Around 5:15 p.m., the climbing team lowered Becca to the base of the route. When the helicopter arrived and landed on the rim, Schaefer considered two options: either lower Becca down 600 feet of steep gully for the helicopter evacuation or move her 200 feet up to where she could be raised.

It had been almost 11 hours since Becca's fall, and the helicopter was the fastest option to get her to critical care. The risk lay in any unforeseeable delay in getting her from the climb's base to the bottom of the canyon. If they took too long, they would need to backtrack, do the Plan B litter raise, carry Becca to an ambulance, drive to Montrose, and so on. The decision was made to lower Becca. It was a tense race against time. The veteran climbing/SAR team had less than an hour to complete a complex 600-foot lower that involved the time-consuming task of passing two knots.

They made it with little time to spare. Just after 7 p.m., the HAATS helicopter flew in, lowered the hoist, and departed with the injured climber.

From the Montrose airport, the injured climber was transferred to St. Mary's Regional Hospital in Grand Junction. Besides her brain injury, Becca's injuries included a collapsed lung and several broken bones, including the pelvis, elbow, ribs, neck, and shoulder. She required three months of hospitalization. Her condition improved slowly. Ashton Johnston, *ANAC*'s Western Slope editor, said, "Becca relayed to me that she expects a full recovery."

The Black Canyon Search and Rescue Team training in May 2024. The practice lowering location pictured here was the same one used eight months prior as an alternative to airlifting Becca Steinbrecher. *Jess Glassberg | Louder Than 11*

ANALYSIS

Former ranger and guidebook author Vic Zeilman wrote: "The items in Becca's pack showed that they were properly prepared for a long climb in the Black Canyon: clothing, food, water, headlamps, etc. They carried radios with them. Skyeler left one radio with Becca and brought the other with him to the rim. Although it ultimately didn't matter because she was unconscious, it could have played an important role.

"One item that could have been very beneficial would have been a SPOT device or something similar. There is no cell phone service in the Black Canyon (or even at most places on the North Rim), so response time can be delayed because the uninjured climber needs to descend the wall, then hike back out to the rim to call for help. Although a SPOT device is not guaranteed to work below the rim, I would rather have the option than not. Skyeler and Becca were capable, prepared, had a plan, filled out a permit, etc. The accident was just the luck of the draw when dealing with climbing in the Black Canyon."

Becca wrote to *ANAC* about the lessons she learned:

- Always do multi-pitch with a satellite device that texts (calls are spotty in the Black) to speed up rescue time.
- Fund and support SAR.
- Wear a helmet. Mine saved my life.
- Learn self-rescue skills. Do refreshers and know the local SAR contact wherever you go.
- The Black is chossy. This route has many reports of loose rock. Climbing is dangerous, rock breaks sometimes. *(Sources: Tom Schaefer, Vic Zeilman, Climbing .com, Becca Steinbrecher, Grand Junction Daily Sentinel, and the Editors.)*

LEADER FALL ON ROCK | Off Route, Loose Rock, Protection Pulled
Glenwood Canyon, Grizzly Creek Wall

On November 11, Cory Jones and I, Max Conway (23), went to climb Mudflap Girl (10 pitches, 5.10+) on the Grizzly Creek Wall (a.k.a. Mudwall). We knew it was to be a chossy climb that entices the adventure seeker.

The approach was not straightforward, and we began climbing around 10 a.m., a bit later than we had wanted. Cory is much stronger than I am, so we planned to break up the pitches accordingly. The first pitch was mine, and Cory had the next three. Soon, it was my turn to lead the fifth pitch.

The belay was a large ledge with two bolts. Mountain Project said, "Angle up and right to two bolts on the face then trend left to the belay." We could not see the bolts. About ten feet off the belay, I placed a 0.4 Friend, which I felt was solid. A bit later, I placed a number 2 Friend that did not feel great. It was in a horizontal crack and slightly over-cammed in poor rock. The climbing was 5.9, so I felt relatively confident. I remember yelling down to Cory, "I should find more pro, but we're burning daylight!" Since Mountain Project mentioned two bolts in my near future, I figured it wouldn't be long before I was safe.

I didn't find the bolts. Before I knew it, something broke. I vaguely remember it being a handhold, but I am not certain. I had climbed about five to ten feet above the number 2 Friend. Unfortunately, it failed and I fell 30 feet. I decked on the belay ledge and bounced off, falling about ten feet past Cory. The 0.4 Friend held.

I was unconscious for about two minutes. After coming to, I asked Cory how I had fallen so far. Then, I told Cory not to make an SOS call and that I would walk it off, we would bail, and it would be fine. Cory instructed me to climb up to him. When I tried, I couldn't move. I was in agony. Any sort of movement in my midsection caused intense pain. I knew I was in trouble. Cory fixed the rope and came down to me. He grabbed my inReach and initiated SOS.

Somehow we also had cell service on the ledge. We were contacted by 911 and by Garmin operators. They assured us that a rescue was coming. Four and a half hours later, the Army National Guard helicopter arrived. They lowered a crewman. After ensuring I wasn't in grave danger, he yelled, "I know you're in a lot of f***ing pain right now, but I need you to get off your a** so I can get this harness under you!" I let out a scream and did what he said. He secured me and off we went, dangling from the aircraft. I had sustained multiple pelvic fractures and two rib fractures. The pelvic fractures required surgery.

ANALYSIS

Our late start influenced my decision to place gear sparsely. I knew the danger and chose to ignore it. While there weren't obvious placements for gear, I could have taken the time to get creative.

Also, I had only been climbing for a little over three years. This accident could have happened to anyone, but I think my inexperience allowed me to ignore the risk. There was some detachment from how dangerous climbing really is.

Looking back, I had begun to follow a line that was off route. After conversations with the one of the first ascensionists, I learned that the route-finding here stumps many.

Despite my mistakes, I did a lot right. I was wearing a helmet, which may have saved me from a serious blow to the head. Additionally, my inReach allowed us to expedite the rescue. Though it's not a "get out of jail free card," it definitely saved me from more time on the wall. *(Source: Max Conway.)*

FREE SOLO FALL
Rocky Mountain National Park, Ypsilon Mountain

On July 9, 26-year-old Bailee Mulholland fell approximately 500 feet while free soloing on the Blitzen Ridge (II 5.4) on Ypsilon Mountain. She did not survive the fall.

At the time of the accident, Mulholland and her partner, a 27-year-old male, were traversing the Four Aces; climbing around and over these towers provides the technical cruxes of the route. At some point in this section, Mulholland slipped and fell.

Ypsilon Mountain, a 13,514-foot peak in northern Rocky Mountain National Park. The prominent ridge rising to the summit was the site of a free solo death in July 2023. Yellow circle marks the accident location. **Christian Collins | Wikimedia**

Her partner called park rangers on his cell phone. He was rescued uninjured by a Colorado Air National Guard helicopter. Mulholland's body was located the next day by the Rocky Mountain National Park Search and Rescue Team.

ANALYSIS

An ongoing trend has blurred the line between ultra-running and technical climbing, often involving large volumes of unroped scrambling over lower-5th-class terrain. Mulholland had significant scrambling and climbing experience, but, as always, exposure to risk grows the longer one is unroped. It's also important to know that an alpine environment, as found on Ypsilon Mountain—the summit is at 13,514 feet—has more loose, dirty, and wet rock than lower climbing venues. As always, climb with more caution in the mountains. *(Source: National Park Service.)*

STRANDED | Unprepared, Unable to Self-Rescue
Rocky Mountain National Park, Longs Peak

On the evening of July 11, park rangers received a report of two climbers stranded and unable to complete their climb on Longs Peak. Neither party was injured. Rangers remained in contact with both climbers overnight, and National Park Service SAR members started toward Longs at first light on July 12. The two climbers had set out on the morning of July 11 from Chasm Lake and had begun to ascend the Casual Route (7 pitches, 5.10a) on the Diamond. The climbers were unprepared for the conditions and did not have self-rescue or bivouac equipment. Rangers assisted the two climbers, and after climbing to the summit, they all came down via the north face of Longs Peak.

At 14,259 feet, Longs Peak is the highest peak inside Rocky Mountain National Park. For most of the year, Longs is in winter conditions, requiring mountaineering experience and equipment. All climbers should have knowledge of their climbing route, the necessary skills and equipment, self-rescue knowledge, and necessary gear for an unexpected overnight stay. *Editor's Note: Climbing the Diamond has become the aspiration for an ever-growing number of climbers. Although the Casual Route is rated 5.10a, it bears little resemblance to short roadside or indoor routes of a similar grade. Completing an adventure climb like the Diamond requires a long mountain apprenticeship. Being unprepared not only risks the lives of the climbers, but also endangers rescuers. (Source: National Park Service.)*

The quickdraw that failed at Catslab. The carabiner's wire gate is not bent, but rather displaced to one side. When the carabiner was loaded, it must have momentarily opened, because the gate notch shows no damage. Climber 2

FALL ON ROCK | Quickdraw Unclipped from Bolt Hanger
Clear Creek Canyon, Catslab

Climber 1 (35) and I, Climber 2 (29), decided to go out for an easy day of climbing at Catslab on April 1. We were experienced, having climbed outdoors for about ten years each. Climber 1 led Overflow Direct (5.10a) with no issues and left the quickdraws for my lead. I started up and made it up to third bolt without any problems. About four feet above the third bolt, roughly 25 to 30 feet off the ground, I fell when my foot popped off. The quickdraw on the third bolt failed, and I kept falling until I stopped less than a foot short of the deck.

I cannot think of anything that either of us did wrong. I believe that, while I was falling, either the rope or my body caused the carabiner connected to the bolt hanger to rotate inside of the webbing loop on the dogbone. The loop crossed the carabiner's wire gate and, when loaded, bent the wire to one side. As it deformed, it released the quickdraw. The flipped carabiner remained attached to the bolt hanger. The remaining carabiner and dogbone came down with me, attached to the rope. I'm not sure I could have done anything differently. *(Sources: Climber 2 and the Editors.) *Editor's Note: There was a similar accident in North Carolina in 2023. For tips on avoiding such events, see page 74.*

IDAHO

LOWERING ERROR | Rope Too Short, No Stopper Knot
City of Rocks National Reserve, Super Hits Wall

On May 26, Brock Anderson and his family witnessed a tragic accident on the Super Hits Wall at the City of Rocks. They were sharing laps on two climbs with another married couple when a group of four young men joined their group. Anderson wrote to *ANAC*:

The climbers had general knowledge of the area, but very little beta and no guidebook. We helped them identify the routes. One of the climbers, Kyle Melby (22), led Twist and Crawl (5.8). My son was reading a book directly under the route as we began wrapping up. I had a premonition that he wasn't in a safe place. I asked him to move 50 feet to a shaded boulder. I thought nothing of it, just a Dad instinct thing.

Kyle was finishing Twist and Crawl, and the two others were preparing to climb Mystery Achievement (5.7), as our group headed out. We were 60 seconds down the trail when we heard Kyle fall, impacting the rock. He'd been lowered off the end of his rope. While we didn't see the fall, we understand that he fell feet-first onto a flake near the bottom. He landed, tilted backward, and impacted the back left side of his head, crushing his helmet and sustaining a horrible head injury. The total fall was about 35 feet. *Editor's Note: An accident in Oklahoma, with a similar outcome, was also caused by a climber falling and being flipped. See page 75.*

The Super Hits Wall at City of Rocks. A climber was lowering from Twist and Crawl (5.8) and fell when the end of his rope slipped through the belay device. His feet struck a large flake (marked with the yellow x) near the route's base. That impact flipped him upside down. *Camdon Kay*

I ran to my truck and grabbed my trauma kit, along with a Garmin inReach. We were able to stop the bleeding fairly quickly, conduct a visual inspection, do a C-spine assessment, and get an SOS out.

It was miraculous that Kyle's only injury appeared to be his head wound. He was belligerent and disoriented (often the case with head injuries). With the help of several other trained first responders, we were able to calm him somewhat, but we couldn't keep him still. Within the hour, a helicopter was on the ground at Bread Loaves and several local agencies were on the scene. They helped transport Kyle via backboard to my truck and up the road to the helicopter. Kyle was flown to Pocatello. We believed he would be fine, but two days later he had died from his injuries.

ANALYSIS

Lowering accidents are all too frequent (*see page 46*). Twist and Crawl is 33 meters long and thus requires a 70-meter rope to allow an interrupted lower while retaining a reasonable margin of safety. A rough calculation, factoring in the length of route, length of fall, and rope stretch, indicates that Melby was most likely being lowered on a rope between 50 and 60 meters long.

Anderson, a licensed raft guide, provided these recommendations after the accident:
- Keep a closed system. Use stopper knots at the end of your rope.
- Speak out if you see an error. I wish I had said something. Some climbers may take offense or feel like you're imposing on their experience, but it is worth going the extra mile. My premonition to move my son from the fall area could have included a friendly question about whether they knew the route was long and that a 60-meter rope might not be enough.
- Learn about where you are climbing. Nuances like long ropes being standard at the City are important details. *(Source: Brock Anderson.)*

ILLINOIS

FAILURE TO CLIP INTO AUTO-BELAY
Rockford, YMCA

In the early evening of November 29, Robert Moresco (38) fell to the ground from a climbing wall equipped with auto-belays.

Moresco wrote to *ANAC*:

"I was new to climbing. The climbing wall was 22 feet high, and I fell about 15 feet. My foot landed halfway on the mat and halfway on a thinly carpeted concrete or composite-like floor. The impact shattered my heel and talus. I had rock climbing shoes on, and I was trying to downclimb when I fell. I think I was climbing unclipped. I was transported by ambulance to the hospital, where I was diagnosed with a fracture of the calcaneous as well as a fracture of the lateral talar body."

ANALYSIS

This type of accident seems to occur at least once a year. It reminds us that forgetting to clip into auto-belays strikes climbing guides, medical professionals, and novices alike (*see ANAC 2023*). Moresco wrote to *ANAC*: "I'd run 3.5 miles before climbing and was fatigued. I feel that there were not enough staff for the number of climbers. Mats were not wide enough, and belay gates did not cover the holds. Maybe climbing walls should be left to dedicated gyms vs. a gym like the YMCA." *(Source: Robert Moresco.)*

KENTUCKY

FALL ON ROCK | Probable Cross-Loaded Carabiner
Red River Gorge, Bald Rock Recreational Preserve

On October 8, I (Climber 1) was leading Grandpa Joe (5.9) in the Red River Gorge. I climbed two feet above the fourth bolt, onto a slight bulge, and announced I was going to take a practice fall. I dropped, felt a snap, flipped upside down, and continued to fall toward my belayer. It was much farther than I anticipated. At some point I hit the wall with my left arm. Both of us were wearing helmets, though I did not hit my head. I stopped five feet above the ground.

We could see that the bolt-side carabiner of the fourth quickdraw was broken and no longer on the wall. I was quickly lowered to the ground and of course was very emotional and crying, as I had feared I was going to deck while falling.

The bolt-end carabiner of this quickdraw broke in a leader fall, most likely when the gate improbably "nose-hooked" a glue-in, rod-stock-style bolt. *Climber 1*

ANALYSIS

The location of the carabiner break could be suggestive of nose-hooking. (I did not know about this possibility until the accident.) All I remember is that I placed the quickdraw in the correct orientation: rubber-gasketed, rope-bearing end down, with the gate facing opposite of the direction that I was climbing.

I wrote Black Diamond and they replied, "The 'failure mode' (looking at where and how the carabiner broke) is indicative of a nose-hook-type failure. We noticed that the wall you were climbing looks like it has fat glue-in-style bolts. Carabiners don't tend to 'hook' onto this style of bolt very easily, but it can happen. It is more likely the carabiner simply became wedged in the bolt, or between the bolt and the rock. Even if clipped correctly, gear can move as you climb past it due to the forces of the rope pulling on it, or other forces. This is a very low-likelihood event, so probably (and hopefully) it will never happen to you again." *(Source: Climber 1.) *Editor's Note: There were several similar accidents in 2023. For tips on avoiding such events, see page 74.*

LEAD FALL ON ROCK | Weight Differential
Red River Gorge, Bald Rock Recreational Preserve

I was getting back into outdoor climbing after a long break. I have been doing a lot of gym climbing over the last six years, including leading 5.11 in the gym. I started getting back outdoors. To optimize my time, I hired an AMGA-certified guide.

On November 18, we had a great day, with me comfortably sport-leading five 5.6s, a 5.9, then three 5.10a/b routes. We then started moving to a different area and walked past Coll (5.10b/c). Although I was tired, the line looked too beautiful to ignore.

Leading the climb, I came off just below the fourth bolt and landed on my ass on the bottom ledge. Pretty sure I fell about 40 feet. I was decelerating by the time I sat down hard on the ledge, which was about ten feet up on the route. I felt a jarring impact and strained the muscles in my back, but that appeared to be it.

ANALYSIS

The 80-pound weight difference between me and my belayer pulled her up when I came off. At the gym, I would have used an Ohm* or anchored my partner to the floor or a sandbag. Despite thinking of the sport crag as an outdoor gym (another mistake), I did not consider the weight differential. *(Source: Robert Bernstein.)*
Editor's Note: The Edelrid Ohm II is the latest iteration of the company's "assisted-braking resistor" device. The Ohm is clipped to the first bolt of a route to increase the braking effect when climbing in rope teams with major weight differences.

MICHIGAN

SWEPT INTO LAKE BY WAVE
Upper Peninsula, Pictured Rocks National Lakeshore

On February 7, James Bake (31) was ice climbing with a partner near Miners Castle Rock when he was struck by a heavy wave that swept him into Lake Superior.

After Bake's partner reported the incident at 5:15 p.m., a search and rescue effort followed. The lake's surface was choppy, with frigid, nine-foot waves crashing into the shoreline. The National Park Service, U.S. Coast Guard, Superior High Angle Rescue Professionals, and Alger County Rescue used boats, floodlights, and a helicopter to search for Bake until bad conditions prevented further efforts. Bake could not be located in the icy waters, and rescue efforts ended that evening. Susan Reece, the public outreach officer for Pictured Rocks National Lakeshore, said, "Bake fell into Lake Superior once, then pulled himself partially back out onto the ice. He was then knocked back in and appeared unconscious to his climbing partner, and then disappeared into the lake."

Without cold water gear, Bake could not have survived for long. His body, located underwater approximately 30 yards offshore, was recovered on February 12.

ANALYSIS

It is not known if Bake was climbing at the time of his accident, but details point to him being unroped. While being washed into a body of water is a rare occurrence for climbers, it has been documented before, and in 2007 an elite free soloist was struck by a wave in Ireland with fatal results. When climbing near open water, use caution and factor in wave height, frequency, and intensity during your risk assessment. *(Sources: National Park Service and ExplorersWeb.com.)*

MONTANA

FALL ON ICE | Collapsed Ice Pillar
Hyalite Canyon

On January 27, Lauren Olivia Smith and Bailey Lasko, both of Bozeman, Montana, were climbing Code Red (WI5) in nearby Hyalite Canyon. This single-pitch ice pillar has a longer approach than other popular venues in the canyon. The approach, combined with the avalanche hazard, made for a more serious outing.

Smith was leading. As she reported to *Climbing* magazine, "[From the approach gully]...the pillar looked funky and off-kilter, in a shape I'd never seen before.... I remember thinking it doesn't look quite right, but the part that was leaning seemed quite big, and we had a big freeze thaw [cycle], so I figured it was well attached."

From a closer vantage, Smith confirmed that the upper part of Code Red appeared attached to the rock and, according to the article, "gave its stability no further thought." At 15 feet up, Smith heard a cracking noise from above. The bottom half of the pillar then collapsed, toppling "like a falling tree." Smith said, "I remember seeing a chunk of ice fall past me with my tool still in it."

The point of detachment was 35 feet above Smith. With no intermediate protection, she—and the unanchored Lasko—"rocketed down the 30° approach slope." Smith had been climbing on the lower-angle (left) side of the formation, and the inclined column fell away from her, so she avoided being crushed. The pair slid alongside the pillar before self-arresting after 100 feet, and they emerged unharmed.

ANALYSIS

Smith did well to assess temperature patterns in the days prior to the outing. She also chose a line that appeared well-bonded to the top of the cliff. While Smith was surprised at the collapse, it's worth noting that the unusual crooked profile and obvious break in the column indicated the pillar had previously cracked and toppled partway, before refreezing at a Pisa-like tilt. Inclined columns are subject to axial compression, shear forces, and, in this case, buckling. Smith says she now completes a full 360-degree inspection of any free-standing ice pillar before climbing. *(Sources: Climbing magazine and the Editors.)*

Code Red (WI5) before and after a dramatic collapse in January 2023. The lower column was clearly leaning to the right, but appeared too big and solid to collapse. The two climbers involved in this accident were fortunately unharmed. *Lauren Olivia Smith*

FALL ON ICE
Hyalite Canyon

Two friends and I, David Baumann (32), were climbing in Hyalite Canyon over a weekend. I followed some WI3/4 climbs and led a WI3 without incident.

On Sunday, February 5, I decided to lead The Fat One (WI3) on the Unnamed Wall since the ice looked plastic on the route. I chose the rightmost line, because it had plenty of rests and was not as steep. My intention was to put up a top-rope and climb the steeper lines on the left.

I started climbing and everything was going well. I found a good rest for my feet and had a solid tool placement just above at hip height with my left and was placing my first screw at about hip height with my right. Either a foot slipped or a tool popped—I fell with both ice tools and the ice screw. I snagged my right crampon on some low-angle ice and felt a sharp pain before landing in deep powder snow.

I ended up with a large blood blister on my left big toe and a cleanly fractured talus bone in my right foot, with several chips from my navicular bone. Several locals assisted in getting me off of the mountain. I was treated initially at an urgent-care facility in Bozeman and was then referred to a specialist. I am very lucky that nothing worse happened.

ANALYSIS

The accident happened so fast, but I must have pulled up on my left tool when I slipped, and in the end both of them popped. (*See photo on next page.*) This was my third season ice climbing, and I was beginning to lead. I thought this route was well within my ability if I climbed carefully and took my time. I think I need more practice placing ice screws and maintaining a stable stance. (*Source: David Baumann.*)

LEADER FALL ON ROCK | Placed Inadequate Protection
Beartooth Mountains, Granite Peak

On August 13, I (Adam M. Clark, 42) was guiding three clients up the east ridge of Granite Peak, a route consisting mostly of broken 3rd- and 4th-class alpine rock, with a few steep, short pitches of low 5th class. The weather was nearly perfect. We were about 400 vertical feet below the summit. I have guided this route multiple times and typically take a belay from clients when leading three or four short pitches. We had just completed a pitch of 5.5, and the three clients were all secured at the anchor. I got put on belay again and began leading up and right on the next pitch (5.4).

We were a little bit behind on time, and I was climbing fast. My belayer had some trouble paying out adequate slack. I slowed down and provided some coaching on feeding rope. I placed a solid cam after 15 to 20 feet of easy ground, having traversed slightly up and right from the belay. Another 15 to 20 feet up, I came to a steep and somewhat awkward move and tried placing another cam. I could not find a solid placement, so I re-racked the piece and kept climbing. At some point I fell. I do not remember the exact moment I came off the rock, nor the fall itself, due to a subsequent head injury.

My next recollection was slowly coming out of an unconscious state. I could not see but could hear one of my clients calling my name. I was struggling to breathe. Slowly I regained consciousness and realized I had fallen about 50 feet and impacted

David Baumann prior to falling off The Fat One (WI3) in Hyalite Canyon (see *previous page*). "I am really shocked that my lower tool came out. This picture shows my position before I fell while placing a screw." In general, it is good to place both tools at almost full arm extension, then place a screw at hip height using the dominant hand while hanging straight-armed from the other tool. Pulling outward on the low left tool while pushing and twisting the screw might have caused the otherwise solid pick placement to pop. *David Baumann*

plenty of rock on the way down. I was now hanging on the rope. I was doubled over in my harness, level with but 20 feet to the side of my clients. My breathing and vision improved as I sat up. One of my clients was texting and told me he had already hit SOS on his inReach, contacted a SAR team, and was coordinating a helicopter evacuation. He told me I had been mostly unresponsive for 15 to 20 minutes.

I soon became fully alert and oriented, and I took stock of my injuries. A large laceration in my left eyebrow was bleeding. Later, in the hospital, I learned that I had chipped an orbital bone in this spot just under my helmet. I had minor fractures on one rib and the bottom left side of my pelvis. My right shoulder was separated. I had a large contusion on my left hip and several lacerations on my legs. The worst injuries were several small fractures to my left wrist; my hand was dislocated about an inch sideways.

The client who caught me had learned to belay only two days prior, during a training session. The one cam I had placed had held. I tensioned off this piece to join my clients at the anchor and clipped in. The four of us were on a very small ledge and crammed into a tight corner. Rescue would be difficult from there, and I decided that we should descend to a large ledge about 65 feet below. Fortunately, a couple of other parties were descending the route at that time, and one of them lowered all of us to the ledge. There we could unrope and tend to my injuries. The Gallatin County Search and Rescue helicopter arrived within an hour and hauled all four of us off the mountain.

ANALYSIS

Months later I still have no memory of the fall and cannot say exactly how I came off the rock. A hold may have broken, or I may have simply slipped. Regardless, haste was a contributing factor. My familiarity with the route led to some complacency. I began to rush and did not protect the pitch adequately. Instead of taking a few minutes to find more gear, I kept climbing, to save time and keep the team moving.

Many non-guided parties solo this route, only using a rope to rappel. Some don't bring a rope at all and consider Granite's east ridge a "scramble." Not that long ago, I skipped belays on similar terrain because I was "comfortable with it." I know many other guides and climbers who have done the same. I am very grateful for taking a belay that day.

I want to thank my client for initiating the rescue on his inReach. We were very fortunate to have that device in his pack, and he made the right decision to call for help right away when I was still unconscious. *(Source: Adam M. Clark.)*

The yellow line shows the route on the upper east ridge of Granite Peak. A) The large ledge below the start of the 5th-class climbing. This is where the group waited for the helicopter. B) This is the location of the belay/rappel anchor at the top of the first 5th-class pitch and clients' location at the time of the fall. C) Approximate point from where Clark fell. *Adam M. Clark*

NEVADA

FALL ON ROCK WHILE FOLLOWING | Rope Stretch
Red Rock Canyon National Conservation Area, Pine Creek Canyon, Mescalito

Joey Portera, Jeff Gerner, and I, Brett Sampson, were kicking off our Red Rock trip with a classic 5.6 trad route: Cat in the Hat (CITH). As a team of three, we've found it most effective to climb one at a time on steep rock. Our plan for CITH was that Joey would lead the first two pitches, with Jeff following and me cleaning. Joey would swap leads with me for the last three pitches.

Joey blasted off and linked the first and second pitches, taking the 60-meter rope up 180 feet (55 meters). Joey put Jeff on belay and he started climbing. Shortly after starting up the first pitch, Jeff fell. The rope stretch sent him for a 10-to-15-foot fall down the broken terrain that led up to the actual climbing. There was enough velocity and rope stretch in his fall to break his ankle in three places when his foot caught a small ledge. His dislocated foot was bent 90° in the wrong direction.

One of the best decisions we made earlier that day was to carry Rocky Talkies. I was still on the ground and witnessed everything, so I was able to give guidance to Joey about how to lower Jeff, when to stop, and when to go extra slow.

Once Jeff was on solid ground, Joey and I talked out a plan. We had two problems: Jeff's severely broken ankle and Joey being stuck two pitches up. He would get down safely, even if it meant lowering himself off a single strand and leaving the rope. There were probably five hours of daylight left, so the clock was ticking.

There is little to no cell service in Red Rock, so I left the scene and headed down the climbers' trail with the hopes of finding service for calling 911, but to no avail. But the texting feature via Apple's SOS satellite service worked on one of our phones (*see page 104 for another Apple SOS rescue*). It took 40 minutes of back-and-forth with the 911 operator, but soon enough, a group of six Clark County Fire Department personnel and a Red Rock wilderness ranger arrived.

They'd hoped to carry Jeff out with a stretcher, but the climbers' trail is narrow, cactus laced, and rocky. A helicopter would be needed. Above, Joey waited until a team of climbers rappelled down and he could descend with them. The helicopter picked Jeff up at 3:10 p.m.

ANALYSIS

A key takeaway for us was that walkie-talkies are worth the extra weight. Being able to communicate kept everyone in the know and brought clarity to an uncertain situation. Also, climbers should anticipate rope stretch for followers. We never considered a "follower" fall injurious, even though there was 180 feet of rope out. Be cautious when linking pitches if it means the follower cannot be seen from the top of the pitch. (*Source: Brett Sampson.*)

When Jeff Gerner fell while following a long pitch in Red Rock, rope stretch generated enough speed and distance to cause a displaced ankle fracture when his foot clipped a small ledge (see facing page). The rugged terrain necessitated a helicopter extraction. Brett Sampson

NEW HAMPSHIRE

FALL ON ICE
North Conway, Cathedral Ledge

On Sunday, January 28, at noon, Ryan Cooper (21) fell about 30 feet while leading pitch one of the classic Repentance ice climb (3 pitches, WI5) at Cathedral Ledge. His fell was stopped by an ice screw and his belayer. Upon impact, his crampon snagged on the ice, which caused Ryan to suffer a serious lower leg injury. He was lowered to the ground by his partner and then was stabilized and evacuated by emergency responders to Memorial Hospital in North Conway. There, he had surgery for a broken leg.

ANALYSIS

Ice climbing poses the usual falling hazards one experiences in climbing rock. Add to this the higher risk of injury due to crampon points snagging on ice, rock, or clothing before the rope stops the fall. Repentance is a steep, narrow ice flow, often candled and aerated, and can be quite technical, depending on conditions. Ryan was fortunate to: avoid a ground fall; have enough remaining rope to allow lowering to the ground; have cell phone coverage; and be near emergency response. Ice climbing should be approached cautiously. Falls, especially while leading, are to be avoided. *(Source: Lt. Bradley Morse, New Hampshire Fish and Game Department.)*

FALL ON ROCK | Protection Pulled Out
North Conway, Cathedral Ledge, Barber Wall

On Sunday, May 28, at 6:30 p.m., Matt Allen (24) was leading Retaliation (3 pitches, 5.9) on the Barber Wall. He took a fall while leading pitch two, pulling out a cam and two lower pieces of gear. His resulting fall was 50 feet and near fall factor two. Allen hit the cliff and suffered serious but non-life-threatening injuries. He was not wearing a helmet.

His partner was able to call 911. New Hampshire Fish and Game Department personnel responded, supported by Mountain Rescue Service, Bartlett Police, and the Bartlett and North Conway fire departments. First responders used the paved state park road to reach the summit area, then some of the responders hiked down to a treed ledge to reach the base of the climb. Allen was alert and conscious, with back pain but with feeling in his limbs. He was stabilized, placed in a litter, and hoisted to the cliff top. He reached the ambulance at the summit parking area by 10 p.m. and was transported to Memorial Hospital in North Conway for treatment.

ANALYSIS

Retaliation's second pitch is a 100-plus-foot-long, continuous, right-leaning crack. While there is good gear all the way, it can be tough to see the placements, since the crack is at your knees much of the time. There have been a few injuries on this climb due to climbers getting pumped, stuffing in less than optimal gear, and then falling from the burly crux layback where the crack steepens.

Allen was aware his cam was marginal but went for it anyway. Lateness in the day and relatively hot weather may have somewhat fatigued him. When possible, take the time and make the effort to find stances where you can ensure your protection placements are solid. In a few spots, you can step down and right of the Retaliation crack to get a good view of your placements and preview the climbing ahead. Solid cam placements generally have lobes at least 50 percent retracted, with the stem aligned with the fall line and a sling long enough to prevent rotation by the rope as you climb past. *(Sources: Sgt. Alex Lopashanski of the New Hampshire Fish and Game Department and Dave Custer.)*

FALL ON ROCK | Wet and Dirty Rock, Protection Pulled Out
North Conway, Cathedral Ledge, Barber Wall

On July 30, we were a party of six trying to crag at Cathedral Ledge after a night of pouring rain. We decided to get a late start to let the routes dry out. Since the Barber Wall is the highest crag at Cathedral and gets sun, we thought it would dry quicker. We didn't find the main trail, but managed to go through the forest and arrive their around 1 p.m. Most of the routes were dripping wet. My belayer and I tried Grim Reaper (5.10d R), while the other four searched for climbable routes.

I roped up and got to a ledge. Ten or fifteen feet up, I placed a green-yellow offset Alien in a dirty, mossy crack at hip level. The smaller lobes of the offset cammed well, but the larger side didn't. I made a few layback moves to an okay stance and placed a terrible number 0.5 cam (both sets of lobes were tipped out) in a downward-flaring crack. I tried to gain the next big layback flake, but the route was dirty, mossy, and wet.

I lost confidence and called "take." My belayer asked if I could downclimb. I could have downclimbed without much difficulty, but I panicked and kept yelling to take.

The belayer took in the slack, but the 0.5 cam didn't hold body weight and popped. The offset Alien also popped, resulting in me tumbling down to the belayer's level. I hit two intermediate ledges and eventually landed on some dirt, rolled, and was stopped by a big tree. I fell 20 or 30 feet. I had a helmet, so the main impact was on my hip and upper back. The belayer wasn't anchored, so they slipped and stopped a few feet from the edge of a cliff below. There was a 200-foot drop behind him where he could have tumbled the whole way down.

We walked out and went to the ER in North Conway. I suffered abrasions, a bruised bicep, bruised hip and chest, and a very mild T9 vertebra fracture. I was able to drive home after being discharged.

ANALYSIS

- After the accident, the staff at a local climbing store said the Barber Wall is the wettest cliff at Cathedral Ledge. We should have asked about conditions.
- I had climbed a wet 5.8 crack on gear without any problem the prior week, which made me too ambitious. I underestimated how conditions affect a climb and the gear placements.
- Onsight climbing on granite is very different from what I am accustomed to— overhanging sport climbs with obvious big holds.
- I could have found better gear placements, especially for the first piece.
- Downclimbing could have saved the day, but I panicked. Being mostly a sport climber, "take" in this case promoted a false sense of security. It made me ignore

how marginal the placements were.

- We might have been able to access the top of this route to set up a top-rope. But getting lost on the approach and losing time made setting up a top-rope seem like a hassle.
- We should have anchored the belayer. *(Source: Anthony Wong.)*

Editor's Note: A well-placed nut is easier to assess and much more reliable than a cam in wet or dirty rock.

FALL ON ROCK | Loose Bolt Hanger
Sundown Ledge, Main Cliff

In the late afternoon of May 28, Jesse Han (25) and friends were sport climbing at Sundown Ledge. He was attempting an as-yet-unnamed and unclimbed route just to the right of Mithras. After scrambling to a ledge, he stick-clipped the first bolt and climbed past it. While working the moves approaching the second bolt, he jumped off, about 25 feet above the ground. When his fall loaded the first bolt, the hanger released, resulting in a ground fall.

Han was able to land on his feet in a small flat spot between boulders. He was conscious but suffered injuries to his lower extremities. The hanger and permadraw that were attached to the first bolt remained clipped to his rope. The bolt stud remained in the rock, and the nut was gone.

A bomber stainless-steel wedge bolt, similar to this, was implicated in an accident when the nut loosened and fell off during a fall. ardour | Wikimedia

Fish and Game officers, Conway Fire, and Lakes Region Search and Rescue responded to the call for assistance at 7:30 p.m. Rescuers stabilized Han and transported him by litter to the Boulder Loop trailhead at 8:15 p.m. Han chose to self-evacuate to the hospital to avoid the cost of an ambulance ride. At the hospital in North Conway, he was diagnosed and treated for a fractured ankle and wrist. *Editor's Note: American Alpine Club members at the Partner level or higher qualify for rescue benefits that may include the cost of ambulance services related to a climbing accident. See: americanalpineclub.org/rescue.*

ANALYSIS

The bolt in question is a solid 3/8-inch stainless-steel wedge bolt in syenite, a granite-like rock type. However, this bolt protects a traverse, and when a climber traverses, the rope may intermittently pull a permadraw at an angle. During prior attempts on the route, the back-and-forth motion of the permadraw had caused the nut to unthread from the bolt. Han did not notice the loose hanger when he clipped and climbed past it.

When using bolts, try to ensure the hanger has not loosened and the nut remains fully threaded onto the bolt stud. Carrying a small crescent wrench to the crag to tighten loose nuts is a good idea. (Several models of nut tools have built-in wrenches.) A local climber involved with establishing the route has since replaced the failed hanger. *(Sources: Lt. Bradley Morse of the New Hampshire Fish and Game Department, Rick Wilcox of Mountain Rescue Service, and Jesse Han.)*

NEW MEXICO

FALL ON ROCK | Off Route, Loose Rock
Sandia Mountains, Juan Tabo Canyon

On November 25, Brian Beyer (male, 25) was climbing with his brother Daniel (male, 27) on the Prow in Juan Tabo Canyon. They began the day at 6:30 a.m., looking to climb one of the unnamed lower-5th-class routes up the formation. They planned to start early and be out of the mountains before dark.

The approach took longer than expected, and they didn't get to the base of the Prow until 9 a.m. After gearing up and selecting a line, they began their climb. After a few pitches, the rock quality started to degrade and the climb started to get harder.

On the fifth and last pitch of the climb, Brian was 15 feet above a number 2 cam when he pulled out a bowling-ball-sized rock and took a 40-foot fall,

The Prow is a prominent formation of not-so-high-quality granite in the Sandia Mountains. Bad rock quality and poor route selection played roles in an accident on November 25. *Anna Brown*

landing in a bush and injuring his foot. Daniel rope-burned his hand while catching the fall. After checking each other's injuries and deciding to self-rescue, Brian decided to continue ascending with his injured foot. They ended up topping out on a false summit as the sun was setting, around 5 p.m., way later than expected.

The team had a windbreaker and a sweater between them, and temperatures rapidly began to drop. After failing to locate a safe descent route, they decided to climb one more pitch to find a better descent. They slowly made their way up the last section (low 5th class) of the Prow and found a rappel station. They were able to complete five rappels on 60-meter twin ropes to reach the bottom. Once there, they slowly made their way to the car, with Brian nursing a foot sprain that required no treatment. They arrived at their car around 3 a.m., after "shivering for hours."

ANALYSIS

Brian and his brother had over nine years of climbing experience each. Brian stated that they both were pretty confident in their climbing ability but needed to be smarter with their skills. He stated that they were overconfident, which led them to begin their climb in the wrong spot.

At the top of the first pitch, they discussed being off route, but decided to push forward, even after encountering deteriorating rock quality. Brian stated they were "trying to convince ourselves we were on the right route." Looking back, he said he would have reevaluated the route and made better decisions on pushing forward.

He also stated that they both should have better prepared by bringing more jackets and clothing to prepare for a worst-case scenario. The warm desert sun in late fall can feel great during the day, making a jacket uncomfortably hot, but as soon as the sun sets and the winds pick up, a clothing system to stay dry and warm is necessary to prevent hypothermia. *(Source: Brian Beyer.)*

RAPPEL ERROR | Inappropriate Use of Prusik
Albuquerque, Ranger Station Wall

On May 5, Climber A was participating as an assistant instructor in a "Climb School" presented by the New Mexico Mountain Club. During a lunch break, she was practicing a 15-foot-long rappel on a single strand of rope using a Petzl Grigri. She had done this previously as a student on another training session, and she was being advised by the instructor for her group.

The Grigri was extended from her harness with a sling. I don't remember the exact length, but the Grigri was within her reach, so it could not have been more than 24 inches. A prusik hitch was applied to the rappel rope above the Grigri. As Climber A backed up to the cliff edge she found it difficult to move because the prusik was catching on the rope. To counter this, she repeatedly fed rope through the Grigri to create slack, backed up until the rope became tight, then pulled the hitch down toward her. This maneuver required her to take her brake hand off the rope. As she backed over the edge with the Grigri's lever open and slack in the rope, she began to fall.

Climber A reflexively tightened her hand on the prusik, causing it to release. Since the Grigri's lever was open, she fell, unimpeded, to the ground. She landed on the upper side of her back. Her head hit the ground, cracking her helmet. Climber A sustained a laceration to the back of her head from the broken helmet shell, hairline fractures to two ribs and three vertebral processes, a partially collapsed lung, several deep contusions, and rope burns on her hand. However, she was able to walk to the responding ambulance.

She spent five hours in the hospital and was able to resume climbing after a relatively short recovery. This accident could have been much worse if not for the short fall distance (15 feet). The residual friction from the Grigri, the hitch, and the climber's hand slowed Climber A's descent. She also landed feet first, which absorbed some of the impact. The ground was flat-surfaced, hard, and slightly down-sloping.

ANALYSIS

The primary accident cause was the use of incompatible techniques that canceled each other out. The Grigri should be attached directly to the belay loop, not extended from a harness. The misuse of a friction hitch as a "backup" eliminated control of the rappel. Simply put, the Grigri, if properly used, is its own backup: If you let go, it stops your descent (see Editor's Note below).

After her recovery, Climber A participated in a club training session on rappelling with a Grigri, using the proper setup and a top-belay from a separate rope. The top-rope belay as a backup for practice rappels is the preferred choice and would have prevented a similar accident in 2023 (see page 79). (Source: David Sweet.) *Editor's Note: When asked about the use of extensions and backups with a Grigri, the company wrote to ANAC: "Petzl does not recommend using an extension or a friction hitch backup when rappelling with the Grigri. Of course you can use a sling extension, but you need to be careful not to extend it so far that it becomes difficult to operate the Grigri. The Grigri attached to the belay loop is easier to operate. Adding a friction hitch below the Grigri will make it quite awkward and tricky to operate the Grigri rappel."

NEW YORK

SHAWANGUNKS ANNUAL SUMMARY
Mohonk Preserve

During the 2023 season in the Mohonk Preserve, there were numerous climbing-related incidents that resulted in either lower- or upper-extremity injuries. Much effort has been put forth within the climbing community to help educate climbers on safe practices and reduce total climbing-related incidents, as well as to reduce the severity of accidents that do occur. When comparing the trend of recent years to that of the last century, these efforts have been successful. Nonetheless, climbing accidents are an inherent risk of the sport, and climbers should exercise the appropriate precautions.

In 2023, there were ten lead climbing falls, two bouldering falls, and one environmental accident that required SAR rangers to respond to climbers in distress. Among these, one incident was due to an environmental hazard and another was due to a musculoskeletal injury. Both of these incidents highlight the need for climbers to be attentive not only to climbing-specific hazards, such as falls, but also to their personal health while climbing and to the environment they are climbing in. *(Sources: Mohonk Preserve Rangers, Dan Cassidy, and Andrew Bajardi, Chief Ranger.)*

SNAKEBITE
Shawangunks, Trapps Area

On May 13, a female climber (30) was on the approach to a climb called Sort of Damocles (1 pitch, 5.8) in the popular Trapps area. The individual was bitten by a copperhead and later treated by SAR rangers. Though snakebites are relatively uncommon, climbers can get bitten if they step too close or do not see snakes. This was the case for the climber. Unfortunately, she also elected to wear sandals for the approach.

In May 2023, a Gunks climber was bitten by an eastern copperhead. This pit viper is endemic to eastern North America and favors deciduous forest and mixed woodlands, where it may occupy rock outcroppings and ledges. *Selbymay | Wikimedia*

ANALYSIS

It is common in the Gunks to find various snakes along approach trails. The 2023 season saw an increase in copperhead activity in the Trapps. Though rarely fatal to humans, copperhead envenomation can cause severe wounds and scarring, especially if untreated at a facility equipped for snakebites. Wearing protective clothing, including pants and hiking shoes, can help protect climbers from a snakebite and prevent injury. *(Sources: Mohonk Preserve Rangers, Dan Cassidy, and Andrew Bajardi, Chief Ranger.)*

FALL ON ROCK | Hypoglycemia
Shawangunks, Trapps Area

On June 13, a male climber (41) sustained a leader fall on Raunchy (5.8) and sustained minor injuries. After the fall, it was determined that the patient, a diabetic, was hypoglycemic. The extent to which hypoglycemia contributed to his fall, or if there were other contributing factors, is unclear. Rangers responding to the incident treated and managed the patient's low blood sugar before addressing and treating the other injuries. The patient required some splinting and care to be safely extracted from the cliff area.

ANALYSIS

Individuals with conditions that formerly might have kept them from backcountry recreation are utilizing new technologies that allow them to venture further outdoors. In this case, a preexisting medical condition may have contributed to a climbing accident. Managing medical conditions in abnormal situations could make the difference between a good experience and one requiring intervention. This could be done through taking intentional incremental steps in any new activity to properly balance your health. *(Sources: Mohonk Preserve Rangers, Dan Cassidy, and Andrew Bajardi, Chief Ranger.)*

NORTH CAROLINA

LEADER FALL | Runout
Stone Mountain State Park, Stone Mountain

On March 5, C. Schmidt (44) and I (J. Eudy, 53) started up Grand Funk Railroad (5 pitches, 5.9-). I was super-focused and led the first (crux) pitch without issue. I brought up my partner, and he led the second pitch. The third pitch gets progressively easier but doesn't have any bolts or gear placements. Instead, it's protected by slinging horns.

I started up the third pitch and climbed 10 to 15 feet above the belay. Before reaching the first horn (protection), I shifted my weight to my right foot and felt my foot slip. I began to slide. At this point I wasn't concerned, since I was on low-angle slab and expected to slide until the rope went tight. Unfortunately, as I slid past the belay, my left foot caught a tiny ledge, twisting my ankle and flipping me on my back. C. did a great job pulling in as much rope as he could, and I stopped six feet below the anchor.

My initial assessment revealed some minor abrasions on my side and elbows, but when I tried to stand I felt severe pain in my left ankle. Within a few minutes, the ankle had swelled and I was unable to weight it, so we decided to bail. From the pitch-two anchors, it was a double-rope rappel to the base. I descended, weighting my right foot only, while C. packed out all the gear and helped me hobble to where we were able to get a ride down to the lower parking lot.

An X-ray and MRI showed that I had a grade 2 sprain (a partially torn ligament), a small fracture in my tibia, and a non-displaced fracture of my talus. I would not consider this fall high impact, and I was surprised at how easy it was to fracture my ankle.

The south face of Stone Mountain with climbers seen on (left to right) Rainy Day Women (5.10a R) and No Alternative (5.5). The historic Grand Funk Railroad (5.9-) follows a line of barely visible "railroad" dikes on the right side of this photograph. It was the scene of an ankle-breaking leader fall in March. *Mike Flint | Wikimedia*

ANALYSIS

This accident was totally avoidable. I was hyper-focused on the first pitch and then mentally shifted gears when I started up the third. In my head, climbing the remainder of the route was easy, and I got complacent. If I had given the entire route the same focus that I did on the first pitch, I would not have slipped and sustained this injury. *(Source: J. Eudy.)*

FALL ON ROCK | Quickdraw Unclipped from Bolt Hanger
Piedmont Region, Pilot Mountain State Park

My climbing partner (31) and I, Alec Gilmore (29), went sport climbing at Pilot Mountain State Park. I have ten years of climbing experience and my partner has six, and we both take pride in our risk assessment and careful approach. The first route we planned to climb was occupied, so we found a nearby route that neither of us had previously tried. We incorrectly identified the route as a 5.7; it actually was Goodness Gracious (5.10a). I quickly realized the route was harder, but I had previously led up to 5.11 at Pilot Mountain, so I went on and clipped three bolts and then hung to work out the crux. It involved throwing a high heel hook and manteling onto an awkward bulge.

I got partially over the bulge and needed to make one more move but couldn't find a good handhold. I ended up falling off. Instead of getting a catch, I hit the ground after falling 20 feet. Both feet landed on a flat rock step on the main hiking trail. My belayer took up enough slack that the rope started to catch right as my feet hit. After lying on the ground, overcoming the initial shock and pain, I realized the alpine quickdraw that I had clipped into the third bolt was still clipped to the rope. Somehow, as I was wrestling with the move, it had come unclipped from the hanger. I was wearing a helmet, but fortunately I did not hit my head or back during the fall.

Alerted by a nearby climber, a team of park employees, other climbers, and volunteers arrived in about 30 to 45 minutes and loaded me onto a transport basket. For the next hour and a half, they carried me back up to the summit, where an ambulance was waiting. At one point, they rigged a rope and hauled me up a steep hill to shorten the journey. At the hospital, X-rays showed I had fractured both heel bones. One of the fractures was bad enough to require surgery, and I received a plate and four screws.

The first mistake we made was not being sure of what route we were climbing. The route I fell from was on my to-do list, but the plan was to warm up with an easier climb. The second mistake was the positioning of the carabiner on the bolt hanger. I knew that it was possible for a carabiner to unclip from a bolt hanger if the carabiner is pulled up in a certain way. I try to keep the spine of the carabiner pointed in the direction I'm climbing. When I was clipping the third bolt, I thought I would climb toward the left side of the bulge. The line turned out to go right, and somehow the quickdraw came unclipped.

Editor's Note: In rare instances, carabiners can come unclipped from bolt hangers. There are several examples in this book (see pages 55 and 58). A few things to consider: The hanger-clipping-end carabiner should be loose in the sling, never held by a rubber keeper. Both carabiners on a quickdraw should be oriented with the gates facing the same direction. As Alec mentions, quickdraws should be clipped so the spine of the carabiner is oriented in the direction of travel and the gates are facing away.

The direction in which one clips a bolt hanger also can be a factor. Clipping the opposite direction from the angle of the carabiner hole will minimize the possibility of the carabiner levering against the hanger and unclipping. Almost all plate-style bolt hangers have the clipping section on the left side of the hanger. So, the ideal clipping direction would be from left to right. Other factors (like the ones mentioned above) may be more important in a given situation, but when you have a choice, this is the preferred method.

For even more security, a safer play is to flip the gate so it opens downward. Better yet, if the clip is critical, e.g., before or after a runout, use a locking carabiner on the hanger end of the quickdraw. (Sources: Alec Gilmore and the Editors.)

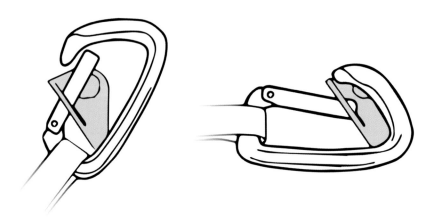

It's an unsettling thought, but carabiners can, on rare occasion, unclip from bolt hangers. When the bolt is clipped from right to left and the hanger angles down to the right, tension on the quickdraw can raise the carabiner and lever the gate open. *Foster Denney*

OKLAHOMA

FATAL LEADER FALL | Protection Pulled Out
Wichita Mountains Wildlife Refuge, The Narrows

On September 22, Levi Wilkins (36), Jake Warren (34), and Jordan Cobb (27) were climbing Leaning Tower Direct (2 pitches, 5.9) in the Narrows. Warren recounted to *ANAC*:

We turned the two-pitch route into three for belay-building and multi-pitch practice. At the base of our third pitch we belayed on a sloping stance (angled 30°). Jordan attempted to lead this final pitch (~45 feet, 5.9), placing a number 2 Camalot and climbing higher and then placed a 0.4 Camalot. He got pumped, lost some confidence, and asked to lower.

I attempted, using the gear that was in place. I also failed and fell onto the 0.4, putting me at eye level with the placement. It wasn't solid anymore. The rope may have caused it to walk. I lowered and I told Levi about the cam. He climbed up while I belayed. He got to the 0.4, removed it, evaluated the rock, and replaced the cam. He climbed above the gear, tried the moves, and fell.

Levi was 15 or 20 feet above us. The 0.4 was two to three feet below his tie-in and four feet to the left. The cam blew out of its pocket. Levi's feet struck both the belay stance and Jordan's head. Levi flipped upside down and backward. The number 2 held and caught him about five to ten feet below the belay ledge. The total fall was 20 to 30 feet, but the tension in the rope accelerated the top half of his body down and backward in an arc. The back of his head (below his helmet) struck the rock. He was unconscious.

Jordan was momentarily dazed from Levi hitting him. The next thing he remembered was me yelling "get him up!" All three of us were wearing helmets. I lifted Levi with one arm, and we grabbed him by the harness and arms. Jordan anchored Levi and helped me lower him until his head was lying on my lap. I angled his head to open his airway. At this point, he took a huge gulp of air. Once Levi was situated, I lowered Jordan to the ground to find help and cell service. Once I had a hand free, I checked my phone. Miraculously, I had enough service to call 911.

I described landmarks and talked the dispatcher through Mountain Project for pictures and descriptions. Fortunately, they were able to get my GPS coordinates. I knew it was a race against time. Having SAR experience, I told dispatch that the only way Levi would survive was if he got helicoptered out.

Levi's breathing was ragged and unsteady. I carefully placed our rope under his shoulders and lifted his chest with my foot up so I could better tilt his head. By then I had found a wound across the base of his skull. I applied pressure with my left hand while steadying his head and neck. His blood ran down the granite. It was bright red and the flow was very slow.

The whole time I was talking to him, even though he was unconscious. When his breathing slowed, I would yell at him to keep fighting. Levi was a Stage IV cancer survivor. I yelled at him that he didn't beat cancer only to die up here. Then, he would take a huge gulp of air. This happened about eight times.

His breathing slowed and became shallower. Jordan returned with two EMS personnel and I relayed everything I could. They told me a helicopter and high-angle rescue team were on the way.

In a photo taken from the team's second belay on Leaning Tower Direct, Jordan Cobb is attempting the third pitch prior to Levi Wilkins' fatal accident. The key 0.4 Camalot placement (behind Cobb's leg) is marked by the yellow arrow. *Jake Warren*

Finally Levi's breathing stopped. The dispatcher told me to begin chest compressions. It was nearly impossible to maintain good form on the incline, but she counted cadence while I gave compressions for two hours.

The chief of the high-angle rescue team had hiked in, and called down from above. He said, "Brother, there's no easy way to tell you this: You can stop giving Levi compressions now." I stood next to Levi's body for another 45 minutes. I dropped the rope to Jordan, and he gathered everything up at the base. The rescue team hoisted me out and an Army helicopter recovered Levi.

ANALYSIS

The rock in the Wichita Mountains varies in quality, and the protection can be tricky and sparse. In this case, the key piece of protection unpredictably failed after holding repeated falls. As Warren wrote to *ANAC*, "Days later, I inspected the cam and it was in perfect working order. The only thing that makes any sense is that the rock around the placement crumbled when loaded."

Placing more protection is usually a good idea, but options were limited. The runout above the critical piece was short, and Wilkins was only ten to 15 feet above the belay. That last fact, along with compromised rock in the key placement, must have contributed to the placement failure. With a short length of rope out, energy absorption is lower. The elevated load applied an unavoidably high impact force onto the failed placement.

That Wilkins flipped, striking his head, was bad luck. Cobb had retreated from the same place, and Warren took a similar fall (slightly below where Wilkins fell) and remained upright. Warren recalled that the inversion "may have been that he hit Jordan harder than the ledge. It was all so fast. I'm 80 percent sure his feet hit the ledge; but the medical examiner reported no injuries to his ankles/feet. They did report that he fractured his C1 and C2 vertebrae." *Editor's Note: These top two vertebrae in the spine are considered a very serious place to suffer injury.*

Unfortunately, getting flipped was probably the fatal factor (*see page 56*). In an article on falling safely, *Climbing* magazine wrote, "The difference between hitting the wall softly and hitting the wall hard can, when you're falling upside-down, be the difference between minor injury or serious injury, life or death." *(Sources: Jake Warren, Jordan Cobb, and the Editors.)*

The Mountain Rescue Unit team lowers Jean Bury down the first pitch of The Cave Route (3 pitches, 5.7 R). During the descent from the summit of Brogan Spire, Bury suffered a severe pendulum fall on the first rappel. *Deschutes County Search and Rescue*

OREGON

FALL ON ROCK | Rappel Error
Smith Rock State Park, Brogan Spire

On August 6, Jean Bury (58) and her husband, Scott, topped out on The Cave Route (3 pitches, 5.7 R) on Brogan Spire. Jean rappelled first from the summit. This diagonal rappel demanded that she walk her feet down an angling groove in order to get to the anchor on top of pitch two. As Jean was descending, she lost her footing. This caused her to pendulum far to the left.

As she swung, the ropes grated over a rock that formed the lip on an overhang. Falling sideways, she landed in an adjacent gully and impacted the rock. She sustained major head injuries to the temple and ear and split her helmet in two. She also suffered a shattered patella, a broken rib, and two broken toes.

Above, Jean's husband called for help and was then able to rappel on her still-weighted rappel line and access her. A park employee and another climber in the area also responded to the location and provided first aid while 15 members of the Deschutes County Search and Rescue Mountain Rescue Unit (MRU) responded. Four MRU members climbed to her location. They further stabilized Jean's life-threatening injuries and packaged her in a litter. They then lowered her down the remainder of the route and crossed an irrigation canal to meet an awaiting ambulance.

This rappel route is known to be awkward and to require route-finding skills to navigate safely. Toby Butterfield on Mountain Project wrote that the rappel from the summit can "be a bit dicey. ...and if you happen to get blown off or fall off while rap-walking backwards towards the P2 anchors, you're in for a big swing..."

There is a newer bolted rappel line to the climbers' left of the angling groove that was established to avoid this exact type of accident. Jean was unaware of this new rappel route, so the pair essentially rappelled the line of ascent, instead of the new descent that follows the fall line from the summit. When rappelling, identifying the next set of anchors from above is ideal but not always feasible. In this case, Jean was initially unable to locate the anchors and created a large pendulum potential by checking around both sides of the fall line. Losing her footing resulted in a swing. Jean was wearing a helmet and gloves, and had a friction hitch in place. These precautions and her husband's quick access and care likely saved her life. (*Source: Caleb Bryce, Deschutes County Search and Rescue.*)

The crux section of Lion's Chair Start (5.10c/d R) at Smith Rock. The higher yellow circle marks the bolt that Genereux was attempting to clip, prior to falling to the ground. The smaller yellow circle marks the location of the number 0.4 cam that pulled out when he fell. *Garrett Genereux*

LEAD FALL ON ROCK | Cam Pulled Out
Smith Rock State Park, Morning Glory Wall

At the end of a great day of climbing on May 15, my partner Lance (30) and I, Garrett Genereux (34), decided to do one last route on our way out of the main area. We stopped at Lion's Chair Start (5.10c/d R). As usual, no one was on it despite the routes on both sides being busy. I had been on the route several times before.

I didn't realize how tired I was until on the route. I was trying to conserve energy by not placing too much pro. I was about one body length above my first two pieces of gear and placed a number 0.4 cam. My belayer asked if it was a good placement. I assured him that it was fine and kept moving. As I approached the first bolt, where the crack pinches down, I became very fatigued and started getting scared. I wanted to clip the bolt as fast as I could. I was able to hang the draw at my farthest reach. Then I pulled up rope to make the clip. As I inched the rope closer to the lower carabiner, my left foot greased off and I fell.

There was a ton of rope in the system, and when I heard the 0.4 plink out of the crack, I knew I was going to the ground. My left foot briefly hit, and then I landed on my butt. I lost my breath and made some guttural noises trying to get it back. I lay supine. My ankle hurt, and my lower back was pretty tight, but I had full sensation and movement below. I even remember feeling like I needed to pee while lying there and took that as a good sign.

The folks nearby were able to clean up the lower pieces, and someone with the longest stick clip I've ever seen snagged the draw off the bolt. Someone let me borrow their camp chair. I was able to slip off my climbing shoes. My left ankle was dark in color and already beginning to swell, but I could bear weight and felt that we didn't need a crew to carry me out.

My partner carried the gear and I used my stick clip as a walking stick as we hiked to the road. I was dropped off at the emergency room in Redmond. My ankle was just a soft-tissue injury, and my back had compression fractures at T12, L1, and L2. I was soon discharged. Subsequent follow-up determined all was good. Two months later, I was back climbing and feeling well. Since then I have even gotten back on the same route. I sewed it with 11 pieces rather than three.

ANALYSIS

Simply put, I did not place enough protection. In the first 15 feet, I only placed three pieces: a nut and a cam protecting the start and then the 0.4 cam that pulled. Also, I could have climbed a bit higher to a better hold and clipped the bolt with the same amount of rope in the system as I had when I fell. I also should have checked in with myself mentally and physically. While it is not the most difficult route, it does take focus and it gets an R rating in the newest guide. *(Source: Garrett Genereux.)*

GROUND FALL | Removed Anchor before Rappel
Smith Rock State Park, Rope de Dope Block

On April 21, Cohen Schaumann (11) fell 40 feet to the ground while climbing at Smith Rock with his grandfather, Scott Phillips. The pair had climbed together on multiple occasions over the prior year. Their sessions included top-roping and a successful rappel lesson. On the 21st, Phillips and Schaumann were climbing on Rope de Dope, a large block with easily accessed bolt anchors that facilitate top-roping. It is a popular destination for climbing classes and beginners.

Phillips and Schaumann climbed some 5.7s, and then the youngster tried and struggled on a few of the 5.9s. They decided to climb Rope de Dope Crack (5.8). Phillips scrambled up the back of the rock (accessed via a ladder) to set up the climb. Unprompted, Schaumann followed Phillips to the top of the rock. Phillips intended only to set up a top-rope, but when Schaumann appeared, the former decided to give him some rappel practice.

Phillips set up the anchor by the book and dropped the rope with both ends clearly seen on the ground. He set up Schaumann on a two-strand rappel with a tube-style rappel device. The youngster was clipped in with a PAS. According to Climbing.com, "Now Cohen leaned back on his rappel device, 'and it looked good,' said Phillips. 'His [PAS] was loose, the anchor was tight, and he had his full weight on the rappel device. I felt good about everything.'"

Phillips climbed down to the ground and circled the block to put his grandson on a fireman's belay. Schaumann appeared to be ready. All he needed to do was unclip his PAS and rappel, something he had done quite recently. Phillips recounted in *Climbing*, "At this point, I walked closer and loosely grabbed the ropes, and took my phone out to take another picture of him. Then I heard a yell, looked up, and he was coming down feet first." Schaumann hit the wall midway down, "and then he went pretty much face first into the ground."

Schaumann had fallen 40 feet, narrowly avoiding some jagged rocks. Because they were at a popular venue, help arrived fast. This included a Wilderness First Responder, a police officer with EMT certification, and wilderness response team in training from Western Oregon University.

Schaumann suffered a broken pelvis, wrist, ankle, and ribs. He had two collapsed lungs, a lacerated liver and kidney, and fractures in two spinal vertebrae. According to his family's GoFundMe site, Schaumann was expected to make a full recovery.

ANALYSIS

When Schaumann landed on the ground, he was accompanied by the anchor slings, locking carabiners, the rope, and his PAS. He had apparently dismantled the anchor before starting to rappel. Said Phillips, "In his inexperience and exuberance to rappel, I think he just unclipped the entire anchor along with his [PAS] when he went to rappel."

In an ideal world, there could have been one person at the top to oversee the rappel and one person at the bottom to provide a fireman's belay. There might even have been a top-rope belay while Schaumann rappelled. Such steps likely would have prevented the accident. However, given that the pair had successfully practiced rappelling previously, such techniques also might be overabundant. It would be hard to anticipate the youngster removing the entire anchor prior to stepping off the edge. *(Sources: Climbing.com, Cohen Schaumann's GoFundMe page, and Centraloregondaily.com.)*

SOUTH DAKOTA

GROUND FALL | Clipped Knot Tails Instead of Knot
Custer State Park, Sylvan Lake Area

On July 4, Person 1 (23) was climbing with two novices in the area behind Sylvan Lake on a wall with accessible top-rope anchors. While setting up the top-rope, Person 1 tethered themselves into a "protective bolt," separate from the two-bolt anchor. They incorporated a quad to build the anchor.

Person 1 moved their tether carabiner from the "protective bolt" and clipped it into several strands of the quad. When they stepped out onto the face and sat back in their harness, they fell to the ground.

Person 1 fell 40 feet. Their momentum was slowed by a large chimney flake two-thirds of the way down and a five-foot slab section at the base. They remained in supine position on the ground while a passerby called 911. The novice climbers used clothing layers to keep Person 1 warm. A SAR team arrived in ten minutes and an ambulance within 20. Person 1 had been wearing a helmet and suffered no life-threatening injuries. They were backboarded to an ambulance, having suffered two lacerations, a large contusion on the buttocks, and a sprained shoulder.

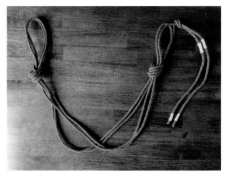

An accident involving a quad anchor system occurred when a climber clipped the loop formed by unusually long knot tails that had been tucked into a knot. When weighted, the tails slipped out of the knot. *Person 1*

ANALYSIS

Person 1 made the quad from aramid cord, tied with a flat overhand knot to form a loop. The loop was doubled over, and two overhand knots formed the legs and masterpoints of the quad. Two long tails extending from the original flat overhand knot were accidentally tucked into that leg knot, forming an unsecured loop. The loop failed when weighted as the tails slipped out of the knot, and Person 1 fell to the ground.

Person 1 wrote to *ANAC*, "My greatest lesson has been to avoid complacency and haste; systems are always worth another double-check. I failed to recognize how a small difference when dressing a knot can have serious consequences. One should tether directly to the appropriate components—in this instance, one of the masterpoints." *(Source: Person 1.)*

*Editor's Note: This incident echoes the practice of tucking a long tail back into a knot or tying an overhand knot in a long tail as a "backup." Most common instances of this involve figure 8 follow-through knots or bowlines. Tucking loose ends or tying backup knots is neither a substitute for, nor a necessary supplement to a clean, well-dressed knot. The AMGA does not recommend a backup to a figure 8 knot because this makes it harder to visually inspect the knot during preclimb checks. In this case, retying the quad or simply trimming the long tails would have prevented a potentially fatal accident.

UTAH

FALL ON ICE | Collapsed Ice Pillar
Duchesne Area, Right Fork of Indian Canyon

On April 2, Meg O'Neill (40), a member of a party of three climbers, was killed when struck by a collapsing ice column on Raven Falls (WI4), near Duchesne in northeast Utah. According to the Duchesne County Sheriff's Office, O'Neill saved the belayer's life by pushing the latter out of the fall zone. The leader was seriously injured.

Sean McLane (34) was on lead near the top of the second pitch when the accident occurred. He was belayed by Anne Nikolov (21) while O'Neill was spectating. McLane wrote to *ANAC*:

"It had been warm for a couple of days, and this was to be my last climb of the season. We were a group of three. Meg was experienced and a regular climbing partner of mine. Anne was new and had climbed a couple of times with Meg." McLane led the first pitch and brought the other two up.

"The second pitch was an ice column that formed at the lip of a cave. It was 40 feet high, 60 feet wide, and 15 feet in diameter. I saw no signs of instability. I didn't see or hear any significant running water. There was little to no cone at the bottom, although a 15-foot radius of ice was present on the ground at the base. I stomped on it to test for anything being undercut, but it felt solid, likely because it was a couple feet thick and my weight wasn't enough to stress it.

"I led out the back of the ice and corkscrewed around to the side. Anne [Nikolov] was belaying, and Meg [O'Neill] was walking around, taking pictures. As I was nearly topping out, there was a significant density change in the ice. It went from wet, one-swing sticks to dense, dinner-plating hits."

McLane climbed above the point where the ice was attached to the rock. As he swung an ice tool into an already dinner-plated placement, the pillar fractured, breaking two or three feet below the point of the pick's impact.

According to McLane, the collapse took "my other tool and both my feet with it. Meg was in the cave behind the pillar, and Anne was to the side. Most of the column went downhill, but falling ice buried Meg."

Sean McLane on Raven Falls (WI4) during an earlier ascent. This two-pitch climb was the scene of a fatal accident in April 2023. *McLane Collection*

Climbing magazine wrote that O'Neill "noticed the ice fracture, and… may have heard it cracking just before the formation broke." She then pushed Nikolov aside. *Climbing* further wrote, "Her quick thinking undoubtedly saved Anne's life."

McLane fell when the pillar collapsed. He recalls, "I had placed screws in the pillar and was pulled off by the rope. The main column fell down the slope away from me, and I came straight down. I hit the ground, landing on my back atop a large chunk of ice. This broke my spine at L2. That was my only injury besides scrapes and bruises.

"I put myself in recovery position as Anne tried to get to Meg. Eventually, I had to decide to send Anne down for help. No 911 calls would go through, and the closest cell service was driving distance away. I showed Anne how to fix a rappel line [to descend the first pitch]. I then gave her my phone and told her where to find my car keys. I took her light puffy to lie on. (I was only wearing a base layer and a hard shell.) Anne drove to town and contacted SAR and local ice climbers. About six hours after the collapse, some Salt Lake climbing friends got up to me. They moved me to where I could be long-lined off. The helicopter brought me to the road, where I was loaded into another helicopter and taken to the hospital in Salt Lake." McLane has physically recovered, and he returned to climbing after about six months.

ANALYSIS

Ice climbing is perhaps one of the most dangerous of climbing games. As described above, frozen water is a fickle, ever-changing medium, and the hazards are often invisible. On Raven Falls, McLane—a very experienced climber who had safely climbed the route twice previously—visually assessed the ice and stomp-tested the base to ensure the column was attached. He wrote to *ANAC* that, "in retrospect, to fail as it did, the pillar must have been melted out from underneath." The solid-looking column was "basically a free-hanging, bus-sized chunk of ice."

McLane notes:

- Running water underneath an ice formation can turn a solid and fully attached flow free-hanging and unstable. Figuring out if ice is undercut can be hard to impossible to do without seeing the running water or the gap between the bottom of the pillar and the base. Several days of warmer temperatures can create this dangerous situation.
- Large variations in ice quality and density on the route may signal stability issues.
- Create a large margin when positioning oneself at the base of an ice route in order to stay out of the way of falling ice. A cave is not necessarily protected if the ice collapses.
- Carry an extra layer. Since it was a warm day, I left my puffy at the base a pitch below. I got very cold lying on ice and not moving for many hours.
- Carry a rescue communicator (inReach) on your person—don't leave it at the base of a multi-pitch route. I now carry one on my harness or backpack strap. (We didn't have one on that day, but it would have been at the base if we had.) *(Sources: Climbing magazine, Sean McLane, and the Editors.)*

FATAL ROCKFALL
Big Cottonwood Canyon, Storm Mountain Island
On May 12 at 7 p.m., Salt Lake County Sheriff's Search and Rescue was called out for two injured rock climbers in Big Cottonwood Canyon. A party of two was climbing Goodro's Wall (5.10c) at Storm Mountain Island when a large rock near the start of the route gave way.

The rockfall seriously injured one climber and killed the belayer. Salt Lake County SAR responded along with Unified Fire, Unified Police, AirMed, and Utah Department of Public Safety. Due to the location of the patients, a technical lowering system was set up and the surviving patient was brought down to the parking lot and flown by AirMed to the hospital.

A climber following the third pitch of Outside Corner (5.7) on JHCOB Wall. The area above him was where Ephraim Cook suffered a fatal leader fall in May 2023. *Chris Farmer*

After the accident, Salt Lake County SAR noted that Goodro's is a well-traveled route that was first climbed more than 70 years ago. But, they warned, after the accident that, "due to the wet, cool winter and spring this season, people need to be aware for the potential of loose rock even in well-traveled areas. Climbers also need to be in the habit of tapping potentially loose holds with their palm or knuckle. A hollow sound will tell you to proceed with caution. The rock that killed the belayer was covered with many years' accumulation of chalk. Beware holds marked with a chalk "X." *(Source: Salt Lake County Sheriff's Search and Rescue and the Editors.)*

Editor's Note: Up to a week prior to this accident, there were posts on Mountain Project warning of yet another "frighteningly loose" block immediately below the anchor chains on Goodro's Wall.

FATAL FALL ON ROCK
Big Cottonwood Canyon, JHCOB Wall

On May 24, Ephraim Cook (25) fell off the last pitch of Outside Corner (3 pitches, 5.7), a traditional route in Big Cottonwood Canyon. Though he had placed five pieces of gear on the pitch, he fell approximately 100 feet and hit a ledge below.

Although the cause of the accident is not known, a police spokesperson said that Cook was properly equipped. The climber's girlfriend made a frantic call to police, alerting them of the fall. However, when crews arrived, the man was already deceased.

Cook's friend Zac Pond said in *Climbing* magazine, "My best guess... is that he made it through the difficult section, placing a reasonable amount of gear, then got up into the easier terrain, where there's unobvious options for gear, and decided to run it out quite a bit."

A failed piece of gear or a long runout might have led to the unusually long fall. Even on easy ground, holds may break or wet rock may be slippery. It is a good reminder that even "easy" terrain can be deadly. It is also a good reminder to know how to self-rescue or escape a belay while multi-pitch climbing. *(Sources: Salt Lake County Sheriff's Search and Rescue, Climbing magazine, and the Editors.)*

GROUND FALL | Inadequate Knot
Maple Canyon, Pipeline

In June, my party of four arrived at the Pipeline in Maple Canyon to find a party of two—a 20-year-old male and a 25-year-old male—already climbing. One of the boys reported that he had just flashed a 5.12c/d. Their combination of strength and inexperience concerned me.

The 25-year-old started up a steep 5.11d. He made a difficult move at the fourth bolt and fell. My wife watched, waiting for the rope to catch. Instead, the climber pancaked flat onto his back from about 20 feet. The rope hung uselessly through the quickdraws, detached from his harness. Writhing on the ground, the fallen climber said, "I forgot to check my knot!"

Thankfully, two of my friends are WFR-certified. They ran to the fallen climber and kept him from getting up. They stabilized his back and neck and sent me to call 911. (Verizon has service at the outhouse near Left Fork in the canyon.) By the time I returned, two ER doctors, who happened to be climbing nearby, had joined the rescue. They performed a spinal examination. The Sanpete County EMTs arrived after about 25 minutes. They gave the patient IV pain meds, put him in a body splint, and extracted him less than an hour after he'd fallen—impressive work for a small-town operation.

Later, we talked to the belayer. The fallen climber had tied the rope to his belay loop with an overhand knot to "hold" the rope while he stick-clipped the first two bolts. After chatting and lacing up his shoes, he started climbing. When he fell, the overhand caught for a millisecond before untying, dropping him to the ground.

Last that we heard, the fallen climber was experiencing lower back pain but hadn't broken his back, as we'd feared. Had he flashed the route and tried to lower from the top, he likely would've died or been severely injured. His head (no helmet) landed within a foot of a suitcase-sized boulder. He was extremely lucky.

ANALYSIS

This accident could have been avoided if 1) the climber and belayer had performed a simple partner check before leaving the ground, and 2) the climber had never tied the rope to himself while stick-clipping.

I don't know if the fallen climber invented this practice or if he learned it from YouTube, but tying the rope to something while stick-clipping is unnecessary. Just pull a few meters of rope through the draw on the stick clip and toss the end on the ground. Please don't add an unnecessary step to a process that's already perfect. *(Source: Creed Archibald.)*

Editor's Note: As Archibald notes, this accident could have ended in death. A 40-year-old female climber died a few months later in Rock Canyon, near Provo, Utah, after falling while tied in with an incomplete figure 8 knot. (Source: Utah County Sheriff's Office Search and Rescue.)

STRANDED | Stuck Rappel Ropes
Castle Valley, Castleton Tower

On December 7, a party of two (ages 25 and 26) climbed the North Chimney (4 pitches, 5.9) on Castleton Tower. Person 1 had three years of climbing experience but was a novice trad leader. Person 2 was a novice. The team brought two 70-meter ropes to descend the standard North Face rappel route. Around 4:30 p.m., the team found the rappel anchors. Concerned about the unusual size of the rappel rings, they tied the two ropes together with a large flat figure-8, backed up with an overhand bend with three-foot-long tails. The unusually large knot was intended to prevent the rope from pulling through the rappel rings.

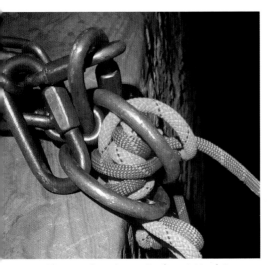

The summit station on Castleton's North Face rappel route features unusual four-inch-diameter rings that dangle over an abrupt edge. Here, the stranded climbing team's large knot used to join the rappel ropes, along with a tangle of long tails, is jammed between the two rings. *Jason Ramsdell | Grand County Search and Rescue*

Each climber did a double-rope rappel using an ATC-style device. Unfortunately, the large knot at the anchor became trapped when it squeezed through one of the rappel rings. The party tried pulling in both directions and whipping the ropes from side to side, but it would not budge. The sun was setting with the party stranded midway up the tower. They had headlamps, semi-warm clothes, and cell service, but neither knew how to ascend the ropes. The nighttime forecast was in the 20s, with possible precipitation. The team decided to call 911 for rescue at 5:20 p.m.

The weather conditions allowed four rescuers to be flown to the summit. The climbers' ropes were found stuck between the two top rappel rings. One rescuer descended to assist the climbers to the ground. They were able to walk out. Unfortunately, the wind picked up, preventing the helicopter from retrieving the remaining rescue team from the summit. The stranded rescuers rappelled the tower in strong winds with poor visibility. Once they were on the ground, the winds briefly died, allowing them to be flown out. They returned to base around 3:30 a.m.

ANALYSIS

Guidebook and local wisdom identify the North Face rappels as the best descent option on Castleton because they tend to be less crowded than the south-side rappels. The sheer face is also less likely to snag ropes. That said, access to the rappel rings requires an awkward transition from the flat tower top to a hanging position below the anchors. It is possible the knot got stuck between the rings as a climber was transitioning over the edge, while they were rappelling, or if one strand for some reason was pulled more than the other. While initiating a rappel, it is prudent to double-check your systems, including where and how the knot joining your ropes is positioned.

A strong, simple knot, like a flat overhand, takes little rope, is easy to assess, and avoids snagging when the rope is pulled. Knowing how to ascend a rope with commonplace trad gear like slings and carabiners is a basic and essential traditional climbing skill.

As a side note, these large rappel rings have contributed to several incidents in recent years (*see ANAC 2022 for one*). Local volunteers have plans to replace these four-inch-diameter rings with standard rappel rings. *(Sources: Person 1, Person 2, Grand County Search and Rescue, and the Editors.)*

VERMONT

RAPPELLED OFF WRONG END OF FIXED ROPE
Wheeler Mountain, Practice Slab

On September 8, Alden Pellett (61) was bolting a new route on the smooth granite Practice Slab at Wheeler Mountain in northern Vermont. Pellett is a very experienced climber, with many first ascents in the Northeast.

Pellett wrote to *ANAC*:

"That morning, I rappelled from a tree to a flat dish, where one could easily stand. There I installed a two-bolt anchor on a route I had rehearsed on top-rope then soloed the year before. I drilled the anchor, equipped it with locking carabiners on a pre-tied quad, clipped in with a PAS, and then pulled my rope from the tree above. I was in a bit of a hurry. Weather was coming in, and I was eager to get the route installed."

Pellett then fixed his rope to the anchor. "I took an end of the rope, tied a figure-8, and clipped it to the quad. The end that I clipped to the quad had a 15-to-20-foot-long tail, something I always try to avoid. The other end of the 60-meter 9.5mm rope lay spread out down the slab, as friction kept it from sliding fully to the ground 100 feet below.

"I put an ATC Guide on the rope and backed it up with a Klemheist knot that was clipped to my leg loop. I slipped on my rock shoes, clipped my equipment to my harness, and began rappelling. I assumed I had 150 feet of rope to work with and was not planning to rappel more than 30 feet at first (in order to assess where to place a bolt). I never double-checked anything or bothered to tie a backup knot as I was sure the rope would more than easily reach the ground.

"Unknowingly, I had clipped into the short tail of rope instead of the long strand. Two seconds after I started rappelling, I felt the end of the rope pass through my backup knot. I had just enough time to look up at my extended rappel device and watch the rope go out through it. 'What the hell!' I thought. I shouted, 'NO, NO, NO!'

"I began falling down the slab. I dropped to my hands, toes, and belly in a futile effort to stop as I began sliding faster. On the way down, I caught my feet on a small, sloping dike and attempted to toss myself past it to avoid breaking a leg and /or wrecking my knees. Tumbling and sliding as the slab eased, I came to a halt five feet above the ground. Screaming from pain and fear, I butt-slid down the low-angle slab to the ground. I had bruised and bloody elbows, hands, and knees. I was wearing a helmet, and a few days later I found deep gouges in its left side. I had clearly hit my head and perhaps slid on it for a bit. I do not recall, but I'm pretty sure it saved me from a bad head injury.

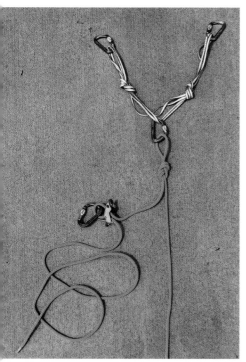

Alden Pellett mistakenly attached his rappel device to the extra-long tail in his figure 8 knot (recreation above). The result was a 100- foot sliding fall. *Pete Takeda*

"That morning, I had parked in the designated climbers' parking lot before taking an unmarked path through the woods to the Practice Slab instead of the established climbers' trail to the main cliff. Unfortunately, my pack with my phone and car keys was up at the anchor. Going up was impossible. I stood up and almost passed out. No one was expecting me home for several hours, and even then, they would not be worried enough to call for help right away. I was basically on my own. I waited a minute or so and stood up again. This time I was able to test my walking ability. I could hobble. I was resolved to walk or crawl out.

"As luck would have it, earlier that morning I had put in a fixed line across an insecure mossy slab that is part of the approach. It would have been impossible to cross in my condition.

"I hobbled down the overgrown trail. Maybe 20 minutes after starting, I finally made it to the dirt road. I found a bent stick to use as a crutch and continued to the nearest house. I started shouting for help. Just then, a car with two tourists drove up the road. There was no cell service in that part of the valley, but the couple was kind enough to give me a ride to a nearby town about eight miles away. Luckily, the county fair was going on and a staffed ambulance was there. Later, I had surgery to repair a torn left Achilles tendon. I also suffered a torn rotator cuff and numerous bruises and deep abrasions, which were particularly bad on my left shoulder."

ANALYSIS

Lack of attention is at the heart of many climbing accidents. In Pellett's case, distraction, complacency, and hurry caused him to deviate from his usual practice of properly dressing his figure-8. This misstep, along with a failure to perform his usual double-checks, led to this near-fatal accident. As Pellett recalls:

"Leaving a tail longer than three feet was something I've avoided in over 30 years of climbing. After several outings of installing bolts and anchors, I had become very comfortable running around on these low-angle slabs. My mother had died two weeks prior to the accident, and I was often filled with grief. Being up on a cliff was good medicine for that new hole in my heart. I guess I didn't realize how distracted I might become."

While Pellett couldn't arrest his fall, he no doubt slowed his velocity, preventing more serious injury. He also showed considerable tenacity and self-reliance in performing a self-rescue. *(Sources: Alden Pellett and the Editors.)*

WASHINGTON

AVALANCHE | Inexperience, Inadequate Gear
Stuart Range, Alpine Lakes Wilderness, Colchuck Peak

At 1:15 p.m. on February 19, a slab avalanche killed three climbers: Seong Cho (54), Jeannie Lee (60), and Yun Park (66). They were attempting the Northeast Couloir of Colchuck Peak in a team of six when the avalanche occurred.

At the time of the accident, the team was traveling unroped on the 1,500-foot, Grade II snow climb. Reports indicate the slab avalanche was triggered by the lead climber and entrained four of the five climbers below. The slide carried the climbers approximately 500 feet down the narrow couloir. All of the falling climbers remained on the surface but sustained traumatic injuries. Unfortunately, for three of the climbers, those injuries proved fatal. The surviving climber, with lower-extremity injuries, was assisted 1,000 feet down to the team's base camp by the remaining two team members.

The team members reported that multiple additional avalanches swept the couloir following the initial slide. These subsequent avalanches buried two of the deceased climbers' bodies. The surviving team members hiked out five miles to make contact with rescue personnel at 8 a.m. on February 20. Persistent avalanche danger made immediate recovery of the bodies unsafe for rescuers.

The Northeast Couloir of Colchuck Peak rises through the center of the face. Four climbers were carried to the bottom of the couloir in an avalanche (yellow circle) in February 2023. Three perished. *Matt Primomo | Northwest Avalanche Center*

ANALYSIS

On February 18, the local avalanche center issued a "moderate" danger rating for the zone surrounding Colchuck Peak. "Moderate" danger (the second-highest of five levels) is defined as conditions when natural avalanches are unlikely but human-triggered avalanches are possible. The avalanche danger was expected to rise to "high" by that evening, and a significant risk of upper-elevation wind slab was highlighted in the avalanche report.

Between February 16 and 19, weather stations in the East Central zone recorded moderate to strong westerly winds. On the morning of the 19th, the party reported light snowfall, becoming heavier as they ascended. An incoming winter storm began to impact the area with increasingly strong west-northwest winds during the afternoon. The winds resulted in blowing snow that likely deposited slabs on lee aspects and scoured windward slopes in the days and hours leading up to the avalanche.

This team of climbers had been in the field, without communications devices, for multiple days and did not have access to this report. Based on subsequent interviews, none of the climbers was wearing an avalanche beacon nor had received formal avalanche training. Three of the four climbers who were caught and carried were not wearing helmets. The survivor was wearing a helmet. While it is not certain how helmets influenced the result of this incident, wearing a helmet provides additional protection against traumatic brain injuries.

A longtime local mountain guide made the observation after this incident that traveling in large groups in restricted terrain, such as this couloir, carries additional risk. Narrow snow climbs are often bordered by rocky terrain that can cause additional trauma and have variable snow depths where weak snow layers can be easily triggered. Climbers should consider avalanche potential and corresponding mitigation strategies before attempting any snow climb. *(Sources: Northwest Avalanche Center, UPI, and Climbing.com.)*

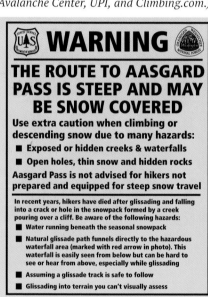

Aasgard Pass has claimed several lives due to falls into crevasses and waterfall holes. Jessi recounted that, prior to her accident, "one climber descending the pass had fallen and severely twisted their ankle, and the week before there was an airlift rescue from the same location." U.S. Forest Service

FALL ON WET ROCK AND SNOW
Stuart Range, Alpine Lakes Wilderness, Aasgard Pass

On June 7, Jessi (30) and Tyler (33) were on their way to five days of rock climbing in the Enchantment Lakes area. First, they had to cross Aasgard (a.k.a. Colchuck) Pass (7,841 feet).

Jessi wrote to *ANAC*:

It was early season and there would still be snow, so we practiced ice axe arrests and got beta from friends who had been in the area the week before. We knew there was one icy/sketchy section near the top of the pass. My pack was around 50 pounds.

I am a slow hiker, so we had planned to take all day to get over the pass.

We were delayed over an hour administering first aid to a hiker near Colchuck Lake. Because of this, we started ascending the pass much later than planned. We reached the sketchy part at 6:35 p.m. We donned Microspikes and helmets and got our ice axes out.

The tricky section required a traverse of ten feet across 40° rock, covered with a thin layer of ice, and then a short step up. Below this section was a steep snowfield ending in jagged talus. Tyler was more experienced and went first. I saw one of his feet slip, but he recovered.

When it was my turn, I was anxious but never thought I would actually fall. My ice axe spike broke the thin ice off, exposing wet rock. My Microspikes did not stick well. I crossed slowly with small steps. I had to decide to either remove my spikes to grip the rock better or just keep going—I left my spikes on. I made sure to use my ice axe for stability, but in the same spot as Tyler, I slipped and started sliding.

I was oriented feet-first, with my stomach down. I hit the steep (40°) snow, got my axe oriented correctly to arrest, but was sliding very fast due to my heavy pack and the slick snow. I tried to push my shoulder further down onto the ice axe, but the next thing I knew I hit a rock and was flipping. I landed in a boulderfield on my back. My head must have smashed into a boulder.

Tyler estimated I slid 50 feet into the boulderfield. I had cuts around my nose and eyes, bruises and cuts down my legs, and more broken bones than my doctors could count. My upper jaw was broken in four places. My nose was broken in two places. Both orbital floors were broken. My sinus bones were broken. My helmet had a huge gash and dent in it—I truly think it saved my life. I think my big backpack protected my spine.

Tyler made it to me quickly. We have both taken wilderness first-aid courses. He used our Garmin inReach to text the sheriff our location, status, my injuries, and the weather conditions. I was evacuated by helicopter at midnight. I was vomiting blood. They feared a head or brain injury, but I did not end up having one.

ANALYSIS

I have thought through this hundreds of times. Should we have roped up? Did we try to ascend in the wrong location? Should we have set up camp midway up the pass and waited until morning for firmer conditions? I don't know if the ice on the traverse would have been any better. After almost ten months of thinking about this daily, I think it was just an accident. I do not think I was too inexperienced. We made good decisions like having first-aid supplies and training, carrying an inReach, and having the right tools to climb snow. Experience told us to be safe and put helmets on. All these factors probably saved my life. *(Source: Jessi.)*

FATAL SOLO FALL
Snoqualmie Pass Area, The Tooth

On August 16, a 35-year-old female climber attempted a solo climb of the Tooth near Snoqualmie Pass. She shared an inReach tracking link with two close friends upon leaving the trailhead.

The climber successfully climbed the South Face Route (330 feet, 5.4) and texted photos from the summit around 6:30 p.m. After leaving the summit, she traveled

The Tooth is one of the most popular summits in the Cascades and was the scene of a fatal solo fall in August 2023. The climber was probably traversing northwest toward the Fang (sunlit spire on the right) when she fell. *Climbing partner of the decedent*

north and somehow fell from the ridge between the Tooth and the Fang (an adjacent summit due north). She fell 600 feet to the toe of the Northeast Slabs route. The climber was wearing approach shoes and a helmet, and had worn rock shoes during the ascent.

One of the people with the inReach tracking information called SAR late that evening after the climber failed to return home and did not respond to phone or inReach messaging. It was also clear from the inReach track that she would have had enough time to return to the trailhead but had not.

A SAR team hiked in the next morning and located the climber's body by 7:40 a.m. using GPS points and drone support. The climber had succumbed to injuries from the long fall. The SAR team extracted the body using a helicopter.

ANALYSIS

Unroped scrambling is inherently risky. The Tooth is a volcanic rock formation, and rock quality varies significantly.

The North Ridge (4th class) is the preferred descent for unroped climbers, but judging from where she came to rest, it was not possible for her to have fallen from that route. Those close to the climber knew she loved traversing ridgelines and was looking for an after-work loop, close to Seattle. An inReach GPS point was sent at 6:55 p.m. from atop the ridge. The next, at 8:05 p.m., was at the bottom of the NE slabs. Sunset on August 16 was 8:18 p.m. Thus, it is likely that, given the daylight remaining, she left the North Ridge descent and crossed onto the ridge between the Tooth and the Fang, with the intent of traversing farther, before descending easy terrain to the west.

The exact cause of her fall is unknown, but loose rock is most likely. When traversing exposed terrain, there is little room for error and caution must be taken to avoid brittle rock and fragile holds. The climber had traversed similar terrain many times and was someone who navigated chossy rock with ease. Her accident was a shock and a reminder that casual mountain outings can be as deadly as more foreboding objectives. *(Sources: A close climbing partner of the decedent, Seattle Mountain Rescue, and Portland Mountain Rescue.)*

WEST VIRGINIA

FALL ON ROCK | Carabiner Cut Rope
Monongahela National Forest, Seneca Rocks

On August 5, a party of two started up Simple J Malarkey (3 pitches, 5.7). The top of the second pitch ends in a corner alcove with overhanging rock above. At the start of the third pitch, the leader, Danny Gerhart (24), placed a 0.75 Camalot just above the belay, before attempting to climb up and left. The leader encountered a wasp's nest and stepped back down to the belay. He then stepped down and to the right on the ramp that ends the second pitch. This was the sequence most used by other climbers.

Gerhart was now about five feet away from the belay. He placed a second 0.75 Camalot before moving up and left to a second alcove, about eight feet above and to the right of the belay. Here, Gerhart placed a number 3 Camalot in a shallow, slightly flaring pocket. (This piece was found with both extended and non-extended alpine draws attached.) At this point, he removed the second 0.75 Camalot to prevent excessive rope drag.

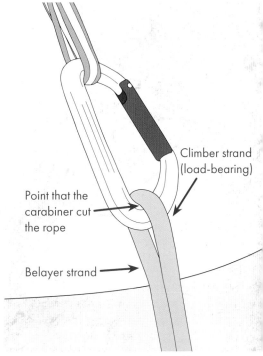

Climber strand (load-bearing)

Point that the carabiner cut the rope

Belayer strand

Gerhart attempted to move up and right from this stance, which is on route. This crux section requires the leader to move out over a roof on a four-foot-high plaque of rock. Though protection is available, the leader cannot see it until they have committed to the crux, and even then, the placement is behind the climber and at waist level. The handholds here could be described as less than inspiring, as water drains onto them from above, adding a polished feel to the rock. Having found no gear, Gerhart stepped back down to the previous stance and discussed options with the belayer.

In this highly unusual accident, the carabiner on the rope-bearing end of an alpine quickdraw appears to have acted like a belay device configured in guide mode. The load-bearing/climber strand (on top) trapped the belay strand (on bottom, under the carabiner) between the carabiner and the rock. The rope was severed. No rock edge was involved in cutting the rope, and no rope sheath material was observed on the rock. *Foster Denney*

By then, the sun was peeking over the top, making route-finding more difficult. The climbing team discussed options before Gerhart decided to move up and left.

Climbing above the last piece and not finding additional protection, Gerhart called down to the belayer, informing them that he was going to take a deliberate fall (acknowledging it was "going to be a big one"). He then let go and fell around 12 feet before loading the rope. The belayer reported having enough time to take in two to four feet of slack before hearing a very loud "gunshot" as the rope exploded. The belayer never felt the falling climber load the belay, and Gerhart fell approximately 130 feet to the ground.

While numerous climbing parties immediately responded to give aid, the fallen climber passed at the scene.

Evidence points to the rope being cut by the carabiner on the extended alpine draw attached to the number 3 Camalot. The carabiner remained attached to the fully extended alpine draw and was found lying on a slabby portion of rock just below the Camalot. Fuzzy remains from the rope sheath were found inside the carabiner. No rope sheath material was found on any nearby rock edges or the slabby rock face.

Photos from the accident scene show about seven feet of rope extending from the tie-in on Gerhart's harness. Three to four feet of core was exposed where the rope cut. The individual core bundles were all severed at the same length; this indicates a definitive "cut" versus extended shredding over an edge.

The third and final pitch of Simple J Malarkey climbs through the overlaps and triangular roofs seen here rising above and slightly left of the prominent cave. This pitch was the scene of a fatal rope-cutting accident (marked with a yellow X) in August 2023. *Krzysztof Gorny*

ANALYSIS

How the carabiner cut the rope is difficult to visualize. But here is my attempt to explain it.

The rope leaving the belayer moved up through the first piece and past the slightly overhanging rock above. The overhang included a six-to-eight-inch-wide V-slot that likely inhibited the belay strand from moving laterally to the right. At the time of impact, the belay strand of the rope would have been lying on the slabby rock face above before entering the backside of the carabiner, which in turn was clipped to the extended draw and number 3 Camalot. In the same way the load strand in an ATC Guide locks down on the belay strand, so did the leader's end of the rope. It wrapped around the carabiner, crushing down on the belay strand and the rock below it, and thus focusing the entire load of the fall onto the small section of rope between Gerhart and the cam.

In essence, Gerhart took a factor-two fall onto the carabiner. In fact, he may have achieved something greater than a factor-two fall, as the pinched rope effectively reduced the rope in the system to around six feet. I'll leave it up to someone more qualified to calculate the force load of a climber falling an estimated 9 to 11 feet on around six feet of rope and all that energy being applied at the bend at the carabiner and onto the belay strand. Needless to say, it was enough to instantly sever the rope.

One tragic fact: It's quite possible that Gerhart's extended sling may have perfectly positioned the carabiner at the time the piece was placed, but then tragically the carabiner shifted into the fateful position. Had the carabiner been just two inches to the left or right, it would no longer have been lying on rock but hanging in free space. Would extending the sling on the first piece Gerhart placed have changed the location of the carabiner in question at the time of impact? This is unknown, as the first piece was ultimately removed by the belayer before they rappelled to the ground, so we were not able to replicate exactly how the rope was running.

Apart from the fact that Gerhart was off route at the time of the accident, this was, in my opinion, a freak accident. Two inches of movement in the carabiner could have made the difference between life and death. *(Source: Arthur Kearns, guide, Seneca Rocks Climbing School.)*

WYOMING

HIGH ALTITUDE PULMONARY EDEMA
Grand Teton National Park, Mt. Owen

At 5 a.m. on June 13, NPS personnel received an emergency notification from a climbing party descending the Koven Route (3,000 feet, 5.4) on Mt. Owen (12,933 feet). A 57-year-old male climber was showing signs of high altitude illness (HAI) and extreme fatigue. The climber was also hypothermic. The climbing party had started the day at 2 a.m. on June 12 and summited at 3 p.m. They had weathered a significant snowstorm while descending.

NPS climbing rangers were dispatched to rendezvous with the patient and assist him to the trailhead. The rescuers arrived at the climbing party's bivy site at Amphitheater Lake at 9:20 a.m. They spent considerable time evaluating the patient and rewarming him with dry clothing, drinks, and food. At 10:30 a.m., the patient was able to start down toward the trailhead. However, his condition continued to deteriorate and he began exhibiting signs and symptoms of high altitude pulmonary edema (HAPE). An NPS litter team was deployed, and they carried the patient the remaining 1.5 miles to the Lupine Meadows trailhead, from which he was transferred by ambulance to the hospital.

ANALYSIS

Although altitude illness is less common in the Tetons than in other North American ranges, the elevations of many peaks in Grand Teton National Park are sufficient to cause HAI. Mild to moderate HAI is often referred to as acute mountain sickness (AMS). The severe forms of HAI include high altitude cerebral edema (HACE) and HAPE. If left untreated, these illnesses can worsen and even be fatal.

The management of HAPE involves immediate descent, supplemental oxygen, and specific emergency medications *(see page 11)*. Of these, descent is the most important. But even with these treatments, as this case illustrates, ill climbers can continue to deteriorate during evacuation. Climbers should be familiar with the signs and symptoms of HAI and react early. *(Source: Grand Teton National Park Search and Rescue Report.)*

Last year, Grand Teton National Park was the eighth-most-visited U.S. national park. The year 2023 also saw a disturbing trend in which technical climbs were listed on popular hiking-specific apps. This contributed to several rescues and a fatality. *Photo of the Grand Teton by Acroterion | Wikimedia*

STRANDED | Inexperience with Snow Climbing
Grand Teton National Park, Teewinot Mountain

On July 14 at 3:45 p.m., NPS personnel received a cell phone call from two young climbers stuck on Teewinot (12,330 feet). The male climbers, aged 19 and 20 years, reported that they were on a snowfield north of the Idol and Worshipper rock formations. They were carrying ice axes but did not know how to use them. They also reported that the snow was soft and they were unable to descend any further. The incident commander coached them on proper descent practices. The climbers then reported over the phone that, despite this assistance, they still needed a rescue.

Two NPS climbing rangers were deployed, and rescuers got to the stranded climbers at 6 p.m. The distressed climbers were lowered on rope systems until they reached the bottom of the snowfield and a dry trail at 7:30 p.m. After resting and rewarming for 45 minutes, the climbers requested that they be allowed to descend at their own slower pace to the parking lot.

There have been multiple similar instances of climbers in the Tetons being unprepared for their objectives, both during 2023 and in previous seasons. The summer climbing season in the range often starts with snow-covered peaks and ends with nearly exclusive rock climbing terrain. During transition periods, climbers need to be prepared for the current conditions and not the ideal conditions.

In recent seasons, rangers have noticed an increase in technical climbing routes being listed on hiking-specific applications and websites. Many 4th- and 5th-class rock climbs with high risk and fall potential are listed incorrectly as hikes. Climbers are reminded to gather their route information from fellow climbers and climbing-specific resources. *(Source: Grand Teton National Park Search and Rescue Report.)*

CLIMBING FALL | Probable Verglas
Grand Teton National Park, Grand Teton

On July 20, the NPS received a cell phone call reporting that a 41-year-old male climber had fallen and was unresponsive. The injured climber had been leading the Owen Chimney feature (5.5) on the Grand Teton (13,770 feet) and had fallen ten minutes prior. The patient, who was wearing a climbing helmet, had been placing a piece of protection when his foot slipped, resulting in a tumbling fall to the belay ledge.

The patient had sustained a head injury, had dilated pupils, and had intermittent breathing. The incident commander relayed initial instructions including rolling the patient on his side, opening and clearing his airway, monitoring his breathing and pulse, and keeping the patient warm. At 11:46 a.m., NPS personnel requested the park's contract helicopter to assist in the rescue. At 11:47 a.m., the reporting climber stated that he was starting cardiopulmonary resuscitation (CPR).

At 12:29 p.m., the party informed the NPS that the patient was still unresponsive, had slow breathing and a pulse, significant bleeding in his mouth, and fixed and dilated pupils. The helicopter departed the Lupine Meadows rescue cache with two rangers at 12:55 p.m.

Unfortunately, at 1 p.m., the reporting party informed NPS personnel that, following 20 minutes of sustained CPR, the patient had died from his injuries. The first ranger arrived by short-haul at 1:20 p.m. and confirmed the death of the climber. A second ranger arrived on scene via short-haul at 1:40 p.m. and extracted the deceased climber's son. The first ranger remained on scene with the climbing partner and began an accident investigation.

ANALYSIS

This team had done many things correctly. They allotted extra time for poor conditions or weather. They researched their route, both at home and at the ranger station. On the day of the accident, the climbers got an early start and progressed reasonably well. They were prepared for the dry conditions reported by others who had descended the previous day. However, on many alpine routes, daily freeze-thaw cycles can coat rock in thin ice (verglas) during the early morning hours. The thin ice was reported in the chimney on July 20 and might have caused the deceased climber's foot to slip.

A fall in non-vertical terrain can have worse outcomes than similar falls in steeper terrain. Per reports, the climber tumbled 40 to 50 feet. This climber was wearing a helmet, but it appears that multiple impacts during the tumbling fall broke the helmet and likely caused further injury.

Following efforts to save this climber's life, two climbing partners were still at the scene. It is important to acknowledge the transition from rescue of the patient to rescue of the partners. First, rescuers should address basic needs such as warmth and hunger. Rescuers should be diligent in psychological care for the survivors. The NPS personnel involved in this incident reported spending the majority of their efforts directed at the care of the two survivors. *(Source: Grand Teton National Park Search and Rescue Report.)*

CLIMBING FALL
Grand Teton National Park, Grand Teton

At 10 a.m. on July 30, the NPS was notified of a 23-year-old female climber who had sustained injuries the day before during a fall, while roped, on the Valhalla Traverse on the west side of the Grand Teton. The climbing party of two was able to self-rescue back to their camp in the Moraines camping zone. Since falling, the patient had complained of symptoms of a head injury, vision disturbances, and back pain. The following morning, when the symptoms had not resolved, the party called for assistance. The NPS contract helicopter responded to the scene with three climbing rangers. Due to the nature of the injuries, the patient was flown to the rescue cache and transferred to an ambulance.

ANALYSIS

This team displayed proper judgment and decision-making following the fall. They made every attempt to self-rescue. The party had traveled a remarkable distance toward the trailhead. They also showed good judgment in calling for assistance once they had exhausted their own resources and realized the patient's condition was not improving. *(Source: Grand Teton National Park Search and Rescue Report.)*

ROCKFALL AND SHORTCUTS
Multiple Incidents and Locations

The 2023 Teton climbing season saw several incidents involving rockfall and climbers taking shortcuts.

One incident occurred on July 30, involving a 26-year-old female climber descending the Southwest Couloir on the Middle Teton (12,809 feet). This climber fell after being hit by rockfall while on a shortcut from the main couloir to the south fork of Garnet Canyon. This is a common shortcut used to avoid traveling to the lowest part of the saddle to the south of the Middle Teton. The terrain is steeper and holds more loose rock than the descent to the saddle proper. A similar incident occurred on September 8 when a 65-year-old male climber fell while also shortcutting the same exit. Unfortunately, this climber was deceased by the time rescue personnel were notified that he had not returned from his planned ascent.

Another rockfall incident occurred in the afternoon of August 11. A 35-year-old male climber was hit by falling rocks while on the Owen-Spalding rappels. Thankfully, before NPS arrived, guides and climbers in the vicinity were able to assist the climber, who was suffering from an altered mental status.

On August 26, a member of a team attempting the traverse from Teewinot to Mt. Owen dislodged a boulder, hitting his 37-year-old male partner. The boulder impacted the climber's lower left leg, and the resulting closed injury showed signs of early compartment syndrome and prevented the climber from walking. Weather prevented a rescue directly from the scene. A climbing ranger was inserted along the ridge to the west at 12:33 p.m. The ranger and climbing partner were able to move the patient to a lower elevation with flyable weather.

ANALYSIS

The similar nature of these incidents caught the attention of climbing rangers. Rescue personnel would like to remind climbers of the dangers both of rockfall and of taking shortcuts. Although rockfall can occur without warning, climbers often miss cues such as melt-freeze cycles or fail to discern areas with poor rock quality. Taking shortcuts to bypass sections of a climb or descent can also take longer than anticipated and expose climbers to more difficult terrain than primary routes. *(Source: Grand Teton National Park Search and Rescue Report.)*

FATAL FALL | Climbing Unroped
Grand Teton National Park, Teewinot Mountain

On August 10, a team of nine climbers were attempting to climb Teewinot via the East Face (low 5th class). Upon nearing the summit, a 47-year-old female climber in the group fell about 150 feet to her death. The team decided to send one climber down to get help, while the rest stayed in place and called for help via cell phone. NPS personnel were contacted at 7:30 p.m.

The East Face of Teewinot was the scene of a fatal fall in August 2023. A late start, a large team size, and reliance on a popular hiking app contributed to this tragedy. *Acroterion | Wikimedia*

After a helicopter reconnaissance, given the late hour and waning daylight, the decision was made to send a ground team to assist the stranded climbers. Four climbing rangers were deployed at 10:30 p.m., and they arrived on scene at 2:15 a.m. and spent the rest of the night with the climbers. During the morning of August 11, three helicopter shuttles brought the rescuers and climbers back to the valley. A short-haul operation then retrieved the deceased climber.

ANALYSIS

Several factors contributed to this unfortunate accident.

- **Late Start.** The team started their ascent in the afternoon, well after most would recommend. An NPS volunteer who was descending the peak at 2 p.m. informed the team of the lateness of their ascent and that other climbers were already descending from the summit. The volunteer also pointed out their lack of necessary equipment to safely continue. Despite this, the team continued up.
- **Large Team.** Having nine climbers in the group likely contributed to this accident. Larger teams always move slower than smaller teams, as rest breaks and decision-making can be prolonged.
- **Use of Hiking Apps.** This team relied on information taken from a popular hiking application, as previously discussed in this section. This climb, in particular, is listed on several platforms as a hike (*see page 96*). Interviews with survivors revealed they were under the impression that the East Face of Teewinot was a traditional hike. It is a 5th-class climb. *(Source: Grand Teton National Park Search and Rescue Report.)*

LEADER FALL ON ROCK | Protection Pulled Out
Lander, Sinks Canyon, Sandstone Buttress

On the morning of July 10, Mac Taylor (25) fell on the first pitch of Gunky (2 pitches, 5.8). He wrote the following account for *ANAC*:

Two friends and I hiked to the base of Gunky at the Sandstone Buttress. I was new to the area. We hiked with gear on our harnesses while carrying ropes and a bag with water and extra gear. I decided to lead the first pitch, despite being told that there was a scary roof section. Part of the reason I chose to lead it was that I already had most of the gear racked on my harness. On the route, I placed a large nut and a number 1 Camalot. I then clipped a bolt and placed a 0.75 Camalot in a shallow slot deep in the crack I was climbing.

Halfway up the pitch, I rested and placed a number 2 Camalot deep in an offwidth-sized crack. I laybacked the crack and got established below the roof. From there, I struggled to find comfortable holds. I was about ten feet above my last piece.

I decided to backtrack. My belayer was pulling in slack while I downclimbed. About five feet above my last piece, I fell. My hands slipped first, and my feet were still on the wall. I flipped upside down and pulled two pieces. The number 2 was a good placement, but it was placed straight in the crack, not oriented in the direction of the fall. It levered out and tweaked the cam lobes. The 0.75 just pulled out. I was caught by the bolt after falling 30 feet. My belayer was yanked up then

Gunky is a popular route in Sinks Canyon that protects well with hexes and nuts. Familiarity with passive gear and more cam-placing skills might have helped prevent an accident that occurred in July 2023. The high X marks where Taylor fell, and the low X marks where he landed. Joe M

dropped back to the ground as the last piece pulled. This resulted in bruising on their elbows and lower back. I split my lip, sprained my ankle, and cut up my left forearm, with heavy bruising on the right side of my abdomen from my harness.

I had stopped right before hitting a ledge. I was lowered to our belay stance, a very large ledge above a slabby wall. My belayer ran down to the car to grab my first-aid kit while I lay on the ground. In the parking lot was an AMGA guide who was also a Wilderness Emergency Medical Technician (WEMT). With their help, we put gauze on my bleeding arm and my lip. We also put a SAM Splint on my ankle. Rather than navigate the entire approach, the guide lowered me down the slabby wall. I walked out with the help of my friends, and we went to the emergency room. I was given a stirrup and crutches for my ankle, and I got stitches in my lip. I had no internal injuries.

ANALYSIS

Taylor wrote, "I think the two biggest factors were my overconfidence and my poor gear placements. I had been warned the route had a scary section, and it was the hardest trad climb I would have done up to that time. I definitely should have let a friend lead this pitch while I took the second, less scary pitch. I also really thought I had placed some good pieces on the climb. I should go back and practice my placements more and get some critical feedback from someone more experienced." *(Source: Mac Taylor.)*

*Editor's Note: The safe use of cams requires education and skill. Employing passive gear on routes like Gunky might be safer and can teach or reinforce basic protection principles. Kyle Williams on Mountain Project wrote that Gunky "can be led with all passive gear...medium to large hexes, a set of nuts, and some tri-cams." "Kyle P." added that there is a "bomber" medium nut placement above the roof where Taylor became fatigued: "Place it before going over.... Just drop it in, tug it, and go."

Mt. Logan (foreground) from the north. Teams entering the St. Elias Mountains must be self-sufficient. Logan can go for years without a successful ascent. The King Trench route, scene of a May 2023 rescue, ascends from the right. *Jack French | Wikimedia*

CANADA

FROSTBITE | Fatigue, Lack of Hydration and Nutrition
Yukon, Kluane National Park and Reserve, Mt. Logan

In late May, a group of three was attempting to climb King Trench (aka King's Trench), the most frequented route up Mt. Logan (5,959 meters). Mt. Logan is the highest peak in Canada. This area of Kluane National Park and Reserve (KNPR) is known for harsh weather and its remote locale. The nearest airstrip is 150 kilometers away. King Trench is a ski-mountaineering objective that includes complex glacier travel. It takes most parties two to three weeks to complete, depending on weather and speed of acclimatization.

This group was at a high camp known as the Football Field (4,900 meters), generally the final camp before a summit attempt. Summit day is a committing 18-kilometer round trip. It requires climbers to go up and over Prospector's Col (about 5,400 meters) and make a long traverse of the summit plateau to reach the top. Summit day requires excellent weather to complete safely.

The group of three had been stuck in bad weather for several days. As the weather started to clear late in the day on May 28, the team decided to make a resupply trip down to their food cache at King Col (about 4,100m). The team completed the trip and returned to high camp at 1 a.m. They were cold and exhausted, and immediately hopped in their sleeping bags to fall asleep. The next morning, one member had frostbite on most of their fingers and some of their toes. The climber was in pain and was unable to travel under their own power without causing further damage. They decided to contact KNPR Visitor Safety.

On May 29, the Visitor Safety team was notified of the need to evacuate the climber. The forecast called for clearing weather the next day. Three members of the Visitor Safety team were on a training and acclimatization trip on Mt. Steele, 60 kilometers northeast. Early on the morning of May 30, two helicopters picked up the Mt. Steele team, and they established a staging area at a base camp on King Trench. The weather was perfect, with clear conditions and light winds. The forecast called for a chance of afternoon buildup, so there was some urgency to complete the rescue early in the day.

The team did a recon of the rescue site and prepared to heli-sling a rescuer to the Football Field. A heli-sling rescue involves attaching a rescuer to the helicopter with a 30-meter line and flying suspended below the aircraft. This allows the helicopter to fly in clearer air and avoid a risky landing at high altitude.

The climbing party was told to dress the injured climber in their warmest clothes, cover all exposed skin, and prepare them to be quickly harnessed and clipped into the sling line. Upon arrival, a rescuer harnessed the patient and they were both slung down to base camp. The injured climber was assessed and transferred to a second helicopter. They were then flown to the Whitehorse Hospital frostbite clinic.

ANALYSIS

A heli-sling mission at 4,900 meters is near any helicopter's altitude limit. Weather conditions were ideal, and the rescue team had recently completed their annual high-altitude heli-sling training. The rescued climber was very fortunate, crediting their recovery to the evacuation speed and excellent care at the Whitehorse clinic.

The frostbitten climber had several learning points. First, the team got colder than anticipated during the half hour spent packing up camp at King Col. They put on heavy mittens to warm up, but the mittens were bulky and did not allow enough dexterity to keep their hands moving and blood flowing. Second, upon their return to camp, exhaustion drove them into their sleeping bags without taking time to eat, rehydrate, and make hot-water bottles. Although it did not feel cold enough for frostbite, exhaustion and altitude rendered them unaware of the cold and the rapid onset of frostbite.

The injured climber had moderate to severe frostbite on nine fingers and two toes. Thanks to efficient rescue and effective treatment, they did not require amputation and have retained full function. Though issues with pain and hypersensitivity remain, they are hopeful of improvement.

This party was lucky to get a good weather window the day after the injury occurred. In this mountain range, it is not uncommon to wait for weeks for adequate weather conditions required to perform such a rescue. (Source: Ian Jackson, Parks Canada.)

The Chinese Puzzle Wall, illuminated above, was the scene of an iPhone SOS rescue in September 2023. Tricky route-finding, loose rock, and pulled protection factored into an accident that struck two world-class climbers. On serious and remote adventure routes, some risks are unavoidable. *Kieran Brownie*

LEADER FALL | Off Route, Loose Rock
British Columbia, North Cascades, Chinese Puzzle Wall

On the evening of August 31, Ines Papert and Emilie Pellerin began a six-hour approach to the Chinese Puzzle Wall in southwestern British Columbia. According to Climbing.com, "Papert realized she'd forgotten her Garmin satellite communicator, but the pair decided to press on anyway, taking extra care to avoid an accident."

Their objective was Crouching Tiger (11 pitches, 5.12b). After a challenging approach including technical, wet slabs climbed while wearing heavy packs, the pair arrived at the base at 2 a.m. They slept for seven hours. Climbing.com reported, "On September 1, they put up and fixed four pitches…jugging up to tackle the second half of the 11-pitch line the next day."

On September 2, they swapped leads, and completed the crux climbing by 6:30 p.m. Climbing.com wrote, "Pellerin began leading up the ninth pitch…(and) realized she was likely off-route. 'I weighed my options, knowing these last two pieces wouldn't hold much more than body weight…. I figured I could pull it off. I did a few pretty hard moves to find nothing but a fully closed seam. This was more risk than I could handle.' Pellerin downclimbed to the highest of the marginal pieces and asked her partner to take. As she weighted the piece, the rock 'exploded in my face.' Her two highest pieces pulled, and Pellerin took a 20- to 25-foot fall."

Pellerin suffered a broken ankle. The pair rappelled and reached the ground at midnight. With a storm forecasted and Pellerin disabled, Papert decided to race to the road to get help. They knew that any delay would hamper air rescue.

Climbing.com reported, "Just before Papert set off alone, Pellerin stopped her." Neither had cell service, "but playing around on her phone, Pellerin had found a button to send an 'Emergency Text via Satellite.'...The pair soon received a message from Apple's support team. They asked her if she had an emergency contact... and Pellerin gave the number of her partner, Ian Middleton. She was allowed... a 40-character message. She wrote: *Call SAR broken ankle 6hour hike Slesse.*"

The next few hours saw confused and frustrating attempts to communicate directly with SAR. Ultimately, the first message—sent to Middleton, along with the stranded pair's coordinates, led to a successful rescue. At 7:45 a.m., a search and rescue helicopter arrived, and by 9 a.m. the pair was airlifted out. Less than two hours later, a four-day storm moved in.

ANALYSIS

Not having proper emergency communication was avoidable. As Papert later said, "I was kicking myself for not bringing an inReach." Friends in the area had satellite communicators, but Papert said she was in too much of a hurry to borrow one.

The iPhone SOS feature saved the day: Introduced in 2022, it allows simple satellite communication versus previous emergency messages that required a weak cell signal. However, this new service has its own issues. Only the iPhone 14 and newer models, are satellite-communication capable. It only works in 16 countries, and it does not allow a direct dialogue with SAR or a dispatcher. The service acts as a third party, relaying a single 40-character message to a single emergency contact. Though Pellerin said that the SOS feature "was so much better than nothing," she added that it is no replacement for an inReach or another full-featured satellite communicator. *(Sources: Climbing.com and the Editors.)*

LEADER FALL ON ICE | Poor Ice Conditions, Ice Dam
British Columbia, Kootenay National Park, Storm Creek

On December 2, a climber was nearing the top of a two-pitch ice climb called Xena (100 meters, WI3/4) in the Storm Creek area. They traversed to establish an ice anchor and broke through an ice dam with their tools. The release of water pushed them off the route, and they fell 12 to 15 meters (40 to 50 feet), breaking their right leg. The belayer was also soaked and lowered the injured climber as far as possible. The injured climber built an ice anchor and rappelled to the top of the first pitch. From there, the belayer fixed a rope to and lowered the injured climber to the ground. They then rappelled down.

A second party nearby heard the injured party yelling and came to assist. They triggered their inReach SOS feature. After the patient was made as warm and comfortable as possible, one person ran to the parking lot for more warm clothing. There they met a Parks Canada warden and were informed that a rescue soon would be launched and they did not need to return to the climb with the clothing.

A Visitor Safety team was slung into the rescue site by helicopter. The rescuers splinted the patient's leg, packaged them in a vacuum mattress, and heli-slung them to a waiting ambulance at the Stanley Glacier parking lot. The patient had a serious tibia-fibula break, mild hypothermia, and vascular damage to a leg, and they experienced compartment syndrome.

Injured ice climber (yellow circle) at the base of Xena in the Storm Creek area of Kootenay National Park. The ice dam that broke, flushing the climber into a long fall, is marked at the top of the route (red circle). *Conrad Janzen, Parks Canada Visitor Safety*

While ice dams with large amounts of water behind them are not common on ice climbs, a significant number of people have encountered this type of event over the years. They generally form on relatively low-angle sections, often at the top of columns or steep ice. Though this hazard may be difficult to anticipate, it reinforces the need to place good and frequent protection, especially before topping out on a route, even if the terrain is easy. Frequent protection can help minimize the length of a fall and reduce the potential for serious injury.

The party had an inReach but had left it in a pack at the base of the route. This led to a delay in calling for outside resources until the second group of climbers arrived. In this case, the delay was not too significant. However, with reduced daylight hours for helicopter response in winter, it's a good idea to keep your emergency communication device with you while climbing. This will maximize the chances of a quick rescue and can improve patient outcomes.

The party was able to get the patient to the base of the route, which helped speed up the rescue. Both the belayer and the injured climber were soaked, and this led to significant heat loss while waiting. The group did their best to put packs and other insulation under the patient to get them off the cold ground. While it may not be practical to bring enough extra clothes and insulation to deal with an emergency, some form of lightweight shelter can substantially reduce heat loss and help with patient outcomes. The more you can insulate a patient from the cold ground, the better.

Sending an extra person out to get more clothing and insulation was a good move, despite this assistance ultimately not being needed. Had any delays in helicopter access occurred, the extra supplies would have made a big difference. *(Source: Ian Jackson, Parks Canada.)*

BENIGHTED | Underestimated Route
Alberta, Jasper National Park, Tonquin Valley, Oubliette Mlountain

On September 3, two pairs of experienced climbers were stranded high on Oubliette Mountain's east ridge (450 meters, 5.9) after inclement weather moved in. The two pairs spent the night in an unplanned bivouac but were prepared with warm clothing and emergency tarps. It rained overnight, preventing them from finishing the route the next day. They were too high to bail off the route, so they made the call to request a rescue. The four climbers were rescued by Visitor Safety staff via a heli-sling rescue.

ANALYSIS

The climbers had more than three years of experience, but they underestimated the difficulty of the climb and may have been off route briefly. They were prepared for a bivouac and wisely requested a rescue in light of the poor weather and route conditions. *(Source: Parks Canada.)*

In the left photo, one can see the twin tracks left by a sliding climber before they plunged into a crevasse. The image on the right captures the steep glaciated terrain and crevasses from a side angle. The rescue team is visible in the yellow circles. *Parks Canada*

FALL INTO CREVASSE | Unroped, Inadequate Equipment
Alberta, Banff National Park, Lower Victoria Glacier

At 1 p.m. on September 17, a solo climber was descending Mt. Collier (3,215 meters) via the Collier-Victoria col. While transitioning from the rocky terrain below the col to icy slopes leading down to the Lower Victoria Glacier, the climber lost their footing and started sliding down the steep slope. After 80 meters, the climber disappeared into an open crevasse approximately 2.5 meters wide, on lower-angle terrain. Fortunately, the incident was witnessed by an Association of Canadian Mountain Guides (ACMG) guide from the top of the Collier-Victoria col. The guide immediately called Parks Canada via satellite phone and initiated a rescue.

The guide (with two clients) made their way down to the point where the fallen climber was last seen. The climber had fallen 25 meters into the crevasse and stopped on a small snow bridge. Surprisingly, they were not badly hurt. The guide rappelled down and secured the climber to the wall of the crevasse. As the Parks Canada rescue team arrived, the guide was just returning to the surface. A rescuer was lowered into the crevasse, and the fallen climber was raised using a twin rope system. The patient was mildly hypothermic and had only some minor cuts and lacerations. The climber was evacuated to a staging area using a helicopter long-line and then flown to a waiting ambulance in Lake Louise.

ANALYSIS

Although the climber seemed to have had some experience, they were not equipped with crampons, an ice axe, a harness, or a helmet. It is believed the climber ascended Mt. Collier via a rock scramble route on the east face, but chose to descend via the Collier-Victoria col. Although this descent option is relatively easy, it involves negotiating steep snow and ice slopes. This accident can be attributed directly to the climber not having the proper gear.

The climber took a very cavalier approach to climbing a high peak in the Rocky Mountains and likely did not research the descent options. The climber was extremely lucky that the fall was witnessed, because they had no means to escape the crevasse on their own. They were fortunate to land on a snow bridge after the 25-meter fall. Had they continued falling, they would have become wedged in the constriction typically found at the bottom of crevasses.

It should be noted that even had the climber safely descended to the Lower Victoria Glacier, they would have been confronted by complex and heavily crevassed terrain without the benefit of proper equipment and a partner required for safe glacier travel. *(Source: Ian Jackson, Parks Canada.)*

Michelle Dvorak and Kurt Ross (yellow circle) await rescue high on the Greenwood-Locke Route on Mt. Temple. This route has seen only a handful of winter-conditions ascents, and Dvorak would have been the first female to join that list. *Parks Canada*

FALL ON ROCK | Protection Pulled Out
Aslberta, Banff National Park, Mt. Temple

On March 23, Michelle Dvorak and Kurt Ross were climbing the Greenwood-Locke Route (1,375 meters, Grade V) on the north face of Mt. Temple in full winter conditions. In summer, the route is given a technical grade of 5.10+, but do not base your expectations on the grade. It has been climbed a handful of times in winter (M6 WI5).

The team was nearing the top. As Ross recalled on Instagram, "I took a long time to climb a loose crux pitch in the dark.... We bivied on a small ledge.... [The next day] Michelle began the next lead block up exposed and runout slabs."

The team was unsure where the next pitch went. Dvorak led up a pinnacle, passing wooden protection from an earlier ascent, but when she reached the top of the tower, it seemed there was no feasible way back to the main wall. She then downclimbed the pinnacle to try another option. As she was making a tension traverse to access another possible line, a piece of protection failed.

As Dvorak wrote on Instagram, "We were only two or three pitches away from the exit ramp when I made the mistake of weighting a cam so as to lower myself down to traverse a blank-looking slab further below.... The gear held at first, but given that the rock was all rather bad, it's not really a surprise that I suddenly went for a long sideways ride, ripping yet another cam and fracturing a few small bones in my back after impacting the wall. The pain was so intense."

Ross wrote on Instagram, "I lowered her to a small ledge then rappelled from my hanging belay to meet her. Considering the mechanism and symptoms of her injury, her reduced mobility, and the difficulty of bailing up or down the face, we decided that contacting parks rescue was the safest option."

Dvorak and Ross used their cell phone to call for a rescue at 3:08 p.m. When the rescue team arrived, both climbers were at a belay anchor on a small ledge. Rescue was able to long-line into their location to prepare the injured climber for extraction off the wall. The climbing party was then long-lined off the wall in two loads.

ANALYSIS

The climbers were very experienced and highly skilled. They had done a significant amount of research prior to their ascent, including reading accounts of previous ascents and studying photographs of the route. In hindsight, the leader felt she could have taken more time investigating and excavating a spine of snow that led back to the wall from the pinnacle. They had earlier assessed this option as unlikely.

One challenge for the party was that much of what they had read about the climb was from summer ascents. The route looked different in winter conditions, adding significant difficulty in interpreting the information. Also, the topography of Mt. Temple is blocky and often nondescript limestone, without the long crack systems and corners that characterize other types of rock. As mentioned in an Alpinist.com feature, winter climbing in general on Mt. Temple "varies significantly from year to year, month to month, even day to day. A winter mixed climb can change from impossible to somewhat casual depending on the conditions." *(Sources: Ian Jackson of Parks Canada, @michelle_divorjaque, @kurtross, Alpinist.com and the Editors.)*

FALL FROM ANCHOR | Tether Clipped Incorrectly
Alberta, Banff National Park, Mt. Louis

At 5 a.m. on August 20, Alistair Hall (34) and I, Adam Laycock (33), started our approach to attempt the Gmoser Route of Mt. Louis. While this 15-pitch 5.9 has bolted anchors, it is also an old-school trad route that would push our limits for climbing on gear. Alistair was confident in his ability to lead the crux pitch. Although it was our first time on this mountain, we were both locals and familiar with the chossy nature of the Canadian Rockies. We did plenty of research and felt confident in the route and conditions that day.

Our ascent was slower than we had anticipated. By the time we reached the top

When Adam Laycock fell free of the fourth-pitch rappel anchor (top arrow) on the Gmoser Route on Mt. Louis, he miraculously stopped on a ledge 35 meters below (low arrow), after tangling in the rappel ropes. *Parks Canada*

Laycock's jammed knot accident was virtually identical to another in Arizona in 2021. In both cases (and in this re-creation), a tether carabiner of the same make and model had a bottom basket flat enough and shaped in such way as to allow a jammed knot to hold weight, if only for a few moments. *Pete Takeda*

of pitch six, it was midafternoon, and with ten pitches remaining, we decided to back off the climb. The belay stations were bolted, so we chose to descend the same way we had ascended. Rappelling pitches six and five was uneventful.

After I finished rappelling pitch five, I secured myself to the anchor with my personal anchor system (PAS). My PAS was a 120-mm nylon sling, girth-hitched through my belay loop, with two knots for length adjustment. The belay stance was narrow, prompting me to shorten my PAS by moving my locking carabiner to a knotted loop closer to my belay loop. I then clipped my carabiner into one of the rappel rings, locked it, weighted my PAS to test it, and took myself off rappel. I spent a few minutes preparing the rope for the next rappel, threading it through the rappel rings, coiling it, and adding a knot for safety.

Then I fell. I was not connected to the wall or rope, and there were four pitches of high-angle terrain beneath me. I tumbled for 35 meters, the full length of the 5.6 fourth pitch. I ultimately came to a halt on a sloping ledge. I was conscious. I screamed, crying out for help from Alistair, who was above me, and the hikers below. Under my legs was one of our half ropes, in which I tied a figure 8 on a bight and clipped it to my belay loop. I yelled to Alistair that I was alive and secure, but injured, and there was no need to descend to me.

My left ankle was visibly disfigured and unable to support weight. Unable to self-rescue, I used my inReach to send an SOS message. Within half an hour of my fall, a Parks Canada rescue helicopter located us and began the rescue.

ANALYSIS

Laycock's accident was eerily similar to another suffered by a National Outdoor Leadership School instructor in Arizona (*see ANAC 2022*). Both fallen climbers had tied overhand knots in a 120cm length loop of 20mm sewn webbing to create adjustment pockets for a homemade PAS. This is a common practice. In both cases, it appears that the tether was not clipped correctly with the carabiner, but instead the knot caught in the bottom, non-gated end of the tether carabiner.

A contributing factor to the accident was that Laycock's daisy knot was bulky from being unevenly tied. This increased the possibility of the knot sticking in the bottom of the carabiner. He wrote, "Despite weighting my PAS to test it, the poorly dressed overhand knot briefly supported my weight." He added, "Before the knot slipped through the carabiner, I failed to thoroughly check my anchorage to account for human error."

It is worth noting that the critical

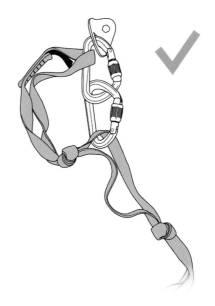

After suffering his near-fatal fall, Laycock wrote to ANAC: "To shorten my PAS at an anchor, I won't unclip the first (longest) loop anymore. I'll clip an additional locking carabiner in the shorter loop, then clip it to the first locker. Previously, and in the case of my accident, I completely unclipped from one loop and reclipped the closer knotted loop." *Foster Denney*

section of webbing was hard to assess. The two strands that created the clipping pocket were of the same color and were flush with each other. Additionally, the rappel station was on a ledge, hampering a full weight test. In the end, sheer luck might have saved Laycock's life.

He wrote, "During my fall, I tangled in the rope, which was still being used by Alistair to rappel pitch five. This might have slowed my fall enough to stop me on the ledge. We had two 70m half ropes that hung 30 or 35 meters below the pitch-four anchor. When I hit the ledge, I was sitting on the tail of the rope, and I was still five to seven meters above the pitch-three anchor.

"Also, my helmet, though it ended up broken, allowed me to remain conscious. Had I been unconscious, I very well might have rolled off the narrow ledge. Considering what could have happened, my injuries were minor: a fractured left fibula requiring surgery, and numerous abrasions." *(Sources: Adam Laycock, ANAC 2022, and the Editors.)*

STRANDED CLIMBERS | Inexperience
Alberta, Banff National Park, Mt. Cory

At 12:20 p.m. on June 13, a party of two requested a rescue from Mt. Cory in Banff National Park. The party was three pitches up a rock route called Hoka Hey! (9 pitches, 5.9) and had just completed a sustained 5.8/5.9 corner pitch. The party felt dehydrated due to the heat that day and their exposure to direct sunlight. Although they had planned to climb in the cool morning, the approach to the route took longer than expected. This delay placed them on the initial pitches of a long climb during the heat of the day.

The party was new to climbing in the area but had recently completed another multi-pitch route called Aftonroe (8 pitches, 5.7), also on Mt. Cory. Hoka Hey! was a step up in grade from Aftonroe, though well within their technical ability. Unfortunately, the additional challenges of a longer approach, route-finding, sustained exposed climbing, mixed traditional and bolt protection, and the heat put them beyond their comfort zone. The party had also dropped a helmet and did not feel confident in their descent options with a single rope.

ANALYSIS

Although the party was capable, they underestimated the length and serious nature of the route. They may have avoided rescue by saving the climb for a cooler day, BY selecting a climb in the shade, or by building experience on smaller multi-pitch routes before attempting Hoka Hey!

There are escape options on the route, but the party was underequipped and did not appear confident in their ability to navigate their way down. It is unknown how much research the party had done before embarking on the route. The climber who dropped their helmet was the more experienced leader, and the other climber was relatively new to the sport. Clipping gear into the anchor and not removing your helmet on a multi-pitch route both reduce the chance of inadvertently dropping equipment. *(Source: Ian Jackson, Parks Canada.)*

MEXICO

FALL ON ROCK | Belay Failure from Above
Nuevo León, El Potrero Chico

On March 14, a friend (the belayer) and I (Liu Yuezhang, 26) headed to Time Wave Zero (2,000' III 5.12a or 5.11 A0) in El Potrero Chico to check out the approach and prepare for a full attempt a few days later. Our plan was to try the first two pitches before returning to the ground. While following the second pitch (95 feet, 5.11b, 9 bolts), I experienced a belay failure from above and hit my right lower back, head, and both elbows as I fell. I was rescued by the El Potrero rescue team and local climbers. Miraculously, I was not seriously injured.

We reached the crag around noon and were glad to meet two female climbers at an area close to our route. They eventually performed the rescue.

I led the first pitch (100 feet, 5.7, four bolts) and belayed my friend up. We switched leads, and my friend led the second pitch, set up a belay, and notified me to follow.

My partner was belaying with a Black Diamond ATC Guide, rigged in guide mode off a bolted anchor. (*See Fig. 1, showing the anchor and belay configuration.*) He had double-checked the system by pulling on the climber's side of the rope. I climbed to the eighth bolt, right before the crux on the pitch. I decided to hang to check out the moves. I said, "Take." I was on the rope for five to ten seconds when suddenly I began to free-fall. I remember the sky moving farther and farther away, so I must have been falling face up. I thought I was going die.

The belayer remembers releasing both hands at one point, after which the climber's side of rope began to run rapidly through the ATC. In a panic, the belayer attempted to hold the climber's rope (rather than the belayer's side) to stop the fall. His right hand got seriously burned. Eventually, the rope (9.5mm, 70 meters, almost new) stuck inside the belay device and I stopped falling in a slabby area, around ten feet below the pitch-one anchor. The falling distance was around 60 to 85 feet.

Fig. 1: This is the actual anchor and belay configuration immediately following the accident on Time Wave Zero. *Liu Yuezhang*

From my injuries, I inferred that I hit my lower right back on a bulge, then struck the back of my head and both elbows before sliding on the slab. My neck and tongue were slightly impaired by the impact. I could not recall some details of the fall. I was wearing a helmet, backpack, and long-sleeve jacket. I noticed climbers approaching on the ground. Then, in what seemed to be the next second, they were above, readying to lower me. According to the belayer, I repeatedly said things like "Where am I?" and "Record the accident scene."

The belayer spent around ten minutes trying to feed slack efficiently after I was connected to the rescuer, but I also did not recall this. My consciousness came back to normal while I waslowered to the ground, but I still experienced some long-term memory loss. The rescue team and local climbers performed a rapid response. I was sent to an emergency room in Monterrey and luckily was not seriously injured. I would like to express my utmost gratitude to the El Potrero rescue team and nearby climbers for the speedy rescue, especially to Juliet, who was one of the climbers we had met earlier and who re-led the first pitch to begin lowering me.

Yuezhang wrote:

"There were a few mistakes made. The most apparent was when the belayer released both hands while belaying. This should be strictly avoided even with an autoblock system. My fall could have been caught if the belayer had pulled on the correct (belayer's) side of the rope; unfortunately, he attempted to pull the climber's side.

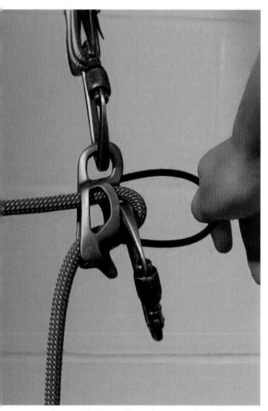

Fig. 2: This shows how the ATC orientation can potentially allow the rope to run through the device in guide mode. *Liu Yuezhang*

"We also tried to analyze the cause of the autoblock-system failure. From the photo of the belay configuration, we can confirm the ATC was set up correctly. (The climber's strand initially was on top but got pulled down beside the belayer strand due to the falling impact.) After some experiments, we found that the autoblock system might fail if (1) there was a horizontal component of force pulling outward (which might have occurred since the belay station was above a bulge, causing the belay components to lie against the rock) and (2) the wire of the ATC was caught by some small structure on the cliff. (*See Fig. 2.*) This scenario is very unusual and, again, can be completely avoided by always keeping a hand on the belayer's side of the rope, but that's the best estimation based on our experiments.

"I was the more experienced climber in the team and the belayer was the stronger climber. To compensate for the experience difference, we held two educational sessions in a gym and completed two local multi-pitch routes together. At El Potrero, we did several multi-pitch routes, safely switching leads, before the accident. I emphasized the importance of keeping a hand on the belayer's rope during training, even while using an autoblock system. As a final note: Always wear a helmet. Mine saved me from more severe injuries." *(Source: Liu Yuezhang.)*

Editor's Note: It is possible that when Yuezhang called "take," the belayer may have grabbed the bight carabiner (or the ATC retaining wire) to disengage the rope/carabiner/device in order to more easily take up slack through the device. While this is not recommended by the manufacturer, it is not an uncommon technique. Yuezhang recalls, "If my memory serves me, the belayer told me he first pulled the slack when I called 'take.'" Thus, it is plausible that the belayer, finding it difficult to pull in slack, disengaged the rope. When the bight carabiner or retaining wire is pulled upward, it also orients the rope perpendicular to the top of the ATC (as shown in Fig. 2). In this case, the ATC might have been pulled horizontally. If the belayer did just that, while Yuezhang momentarily shifted his weight on and off the rope, the rope could have begun to slip rapidly through the ATC.

We know that the belayer, now panicking, mistakenly grabbed the follower's side of the rope in a vain attempt to arrest the fall. His grip may have prevented the device from loading, that is until excruciating rope burns forced him to release the rope. At this point, the rope locked in the now loaded ATC. The newness of the rope also probably played a role. Note that in Fig. 1, the climber's side of the rope is loaded adjacent to the brake side, not on top, as per the intended design. This is probably due to the force of the fall and the slickness/diameter of the fresh rope. Extra caution must be taken when using a thin and slick rope.

FALL ON SNOW | Team Fall While Roped
Puebla, Pico de Orizaba (Citlaltépetl)

On August 20, a fall killed four people climbing Pico de Orizaba (5,636 meters), Mexico's highest peak. The climbers were roped together above 5,000 meters on the Jamapa Glacier when one of them fell, dragging the other three down the mountain.

The secretary of the interior for the state of Puebla confirmed that all four climbers were Mexican nationals and belonged to the same group. Three of the deceased were from Veracruz, and one was from Puebla. The tour company Volcanes de México identified the fallen as Carlos Altamirano Lima (53), José Inés Zepahua (63), Hugo Cruz Vázquez (19), and Humberto Kenji Muray (58). Altamirano was guiding the group and was an experienced mountaineer.

ANALYSIS

The standard Jamapa Glacier route (the scene of the accident) is not technically difficult. However, above 5,000 meters, crevasses present a hazard and the snow steepens to 35°. On hard snow angled at 30°, a falling climber accelerates almost as quickly as they would in free fall.

Although being roped together in a team of varying experience levels is standard for safeguarding glacier travel, it presents various hazards. The general principal is that if one climber falls, their fall can be arrested by one or more of the others. Unfortunately, on steep terrain, this can prove difficult, especially if the top member of the rope team falls. In an ideal world, pitching out technical terrain or having intermediate anchors mitigates the hazard. In reality, such steps often are impractical, especially in situations where speed is safety.

While the uninitiated view "low-angle" snow climbing as inconsequential, experienced climbers understand the danger. Protection is often poor or nonexistent. The chances of falling are magnified by slick terrain, unstable footing, and falling objects. "Balling" of built-up snow on crampons and tripping when crampon points catch pant cuffs have killed many climbers. Self-arresting on steep, hard snow is very difficult. All that said, one must exercise heightened caution and avoid being lulled into a false sense of security when climbing steep snow. (Sources: Government of Puebla, ExplorersWeb.com, and the Editors.)

SKI MOUNTAINEERING

FALLING ICE | Poor Position, Group Dynamics
California, Sierra Nevada, Mt. Emerson

Our party of four planned to ski the North Couloir on Mt. Emerson (13,210 feet), west of Bishop, on May 18. Two members of our party had skied in this area before, but not on Emerson specifically. The other two were visiting from out of state. Three of the four of us are volunteers on mountain rescue teams, and two are current or former licensed EMTs.

The weather was around 40°F at the Aspendell trailhead (8,400 feet) when we started at 5:30 a.m. The forecast was for clear skies and a high of 70°F at that elevation. Our objective topped out at around 13,000 feet, where we expected lower overnight temperatures and a cooler high.

Climbing the North Couloir of Mt. Emerson, shortly before falling ice struck the team. The frozen waterfall that was shedding ice is seen high on the right. *Team Photo*

We arrived at the base of the couloir around 9 a.m. and found a party of three just starting up. We followed shortly after them, starting our climb around 9:15 a.m. One member of the party ahead of us soon descended, and we caught up with the remaining two. Shortly after this, we were hit by falling ice chunks (up to softball sized), and we identified a frozen waterfall about 800 feet up the couloir, on climbers' right, as the source. While the snow surface in the north-facing couloir was in the shade and quite firm, the waterfall was seeing its first sun at the top of the couloir's wall.

We decided we would continue but if a similar incident happened we would bail. Communication of this decision within our party was imperfect due to group dynamics and being somewhat spread out across the couloir. After regrouping in a protected area on climbers' left, we restarted as a team of four while the other party continued 100 to 200 feet above us. Person 1 (female, age 39) expressed hesitation in continuing, partly due to her perceived inability to maintain the pace set by the other climbers. Moving quickly and traveling together were emphasized as tactics for mitigating the overhead hazard.

Around 10 a.m., when we were about 50 feet below the waterfall, it shed more ice and hit our group directly. We estimate some of the ice chunks were microwave sized. None of the party members were knocked off their feet, but Person 1 was struck by ice in the head while she was in self-arrest position, as evidenced by a large dent on the top of her helmet. She was conscious but not alert and oriented, and incapable of climbing farther or descending on skis. She complained of light neck pain, moderate shoulder pain, and moderate hip pain. She was able to move and sense all extremities. Persons 2 and 3 also were struck in their heads, as evidenced by a laceration on Person 3's ear and both helmets showing damage. Neither complained of significant pain or cognitive deficits.

The SOS feature on a Garmin inReach was activated. Persons 3 and 4 continued climbing to get above the hazard; they then transitioned to skis, and one person skied down the couloir to call 911. Meanwhile, Person 2 assisted Person 1 in downclimbing the couloir. Over the next 15 minutes, the injured member's mental status was reassessed as alert and oriented (A&Ox4). She continued to complain of neck, shoulder, and hip pain, but the pain did not inhibit movement and no neurological deficits were observed.

Over the next 90 minutes, Persons 1 and 2 descended 800 feet to a safe zone on the apron below the couloir. The waterfall shed ice at least four times during this period, including once when large ice chunks fell down the couloir.

Inyo County SAR had initiated a call for helicopter resources but estimated they would not be in the area for a few hours and encouraged us to keep moving downhill if we were able. We made the decision to self-evacuate. We skied down the low-angle approach and reached the trailhead around 3 p.m.

At Northern Inyo Hospital, Person 1 was found to have a concussion and fractured C1 vertebra. She has made a full recovery. Person 3 needed stiches for a laceration on the back of her ear.

ANALYSIS

Ultimately, poor group dynamics led to the decision to continue climbing beneath a known hazard. Further, the group did not have enough experience with overhead ice hazard to fully assess the risk and appreciate how little "moving fast" mitigates that risk. Large chunks of falling ice would break up on the frozen snow of the couloir, which meant the potential for harm from large pieces of ice increased as the group climbed closer to the waterfall. The group had several opportunities to pause and discuss climbing strategy, pacing, and overall comfort with the objective, but failed to do that because of an overwhelming sense of urgency to move quickly.

Without observing this specific frozen waterfall frequently, it would not be possible to predict when it would melt and fall apart each day. We hypothesize the waterfall had been going through a diurnal freeze-thaw cycle, fed by a melting snowfield above. A much, much earlier start might have reduced the risk of being in a vulnerable climbing position during the bulk of the waterfall shedding. The sun hits the top of the couloir walls around 6 a.m. at that time of year.

After the incident, the group successfully executed a self-rescue. In hindsight, skiing down 3,000 vertical feet with a fractured C1 vertebra, in excellent weather and with plenty of time to wait for air rescue, was not a perfect decision. The team lacked knowledge of cervical spine mechanisms of injury, learning later that a significant axial load (large ice chunk to the head) followed by immediate neck pain (even minor pain) is indicative of possible fracture. The medical assessments in the field were thorough, but all parties were distracted by the dangerous and stressful situation of falling ice in the couloir. The team's medical training and experience in rescue led to the decision to very quickly self-extricate from the couloir to avoid further injury. *(Source: Person 1.)*

AVALANCHE | Late-Season Wet Loose Slide
California, Sierra Nevada, Hurd Peak

On the morning of June 14, a party of two was ascending the north side of 12,237-foot Hurd Peak when they began to notice signs of instability. Skier 2 reported that they discussed the deteriorating conditions and the possibility of turning around. Soon after this discussion, a natural wet loose avalanche released at about 11,940 feet, about 400 feet above the party, and swept both individuals down the slope. Skier 1 was carried over a cliffband, and both parties were partially buried.

After coming to rest, Skier 2 had a hand free and was able to clear their face, dig themselves out, and initiate a search for Skier 1, who was partially buried with a leg exposed. Skier 2 was able to locate and extract them quickly. After assessing Skier 1's condition, Skier 2 initiated a rescue via an inReach at approximately 11:45 a.m.

Skier 1 sustained critical injuries during the avalanche, and their condition deteriorated with time. The rescue was complicated by continued avalanche threat. During a subsequent avalanche, Skier 2 was forced to retreat from the toe of the debris to nearby safety before returning to uncover Skier 1 a second time.

Inyo County Search and Rescue arrived on the scene in midafternoon, and Skier 1 was airlifted to the hospital. Unfortunately, despite the heroic efforts of Skier 2 and the rescue team, Skier 1 did not survive their injuries.

ANALYSIS

This season's record-breaking snowfall and abnormally cold spring led to substantial snow coverage lasting well into the summer months. This allowed for better-than-usual access for backcountry skiers and riders. It also meant the snowpack was subjected to atypical weather inputs, including intense solar radiation, summer rain and snow showers, and very warm overnight temperatures. This event is a tragic reminder that the snowpack remains dynamic—and destructive avalanches are still possible—during the spring and summer months.

Overnight temperatures measured at the South Lake weather plot (9,600 feet), near the site of this incident, remained near or above freezing for several days leading up to the accident. In early summer, the north face of Hurd Peak receives solar input shortly after sunrise. The shallow nature of this slope and exposed rock features encourage rapid warming. Cloud cover on the evening of June 13 may also have limited the overnight refreeze potential.

It's also important to note that the approach and lower flanks of the north face have a northwest aspect and are partially protected from the morning sun. Snow in the upper start zone thus warms quicker than snow along the approach. The first signs of instability may not be observed until skiers are fully exposed to overhead hazards.

On the morning of the accident, a solo skier climbed and descended the face at approximately 9 a.m., observing signs of impending snow instability, including wet surface snow and deep boot penetration on the climb. This skier triggered a small wet loose avalanche at the top of the path and carefully descended the bed surface. The skier did not see the party that would be involved in the accident later that morning.

Looking up the avalanche path and debris on the north side of Hurd Peak. (A) Location of Skier 2 at the time of the avalanche. (B) Estimated location of Skier 1. *Eastern Sierra Avalanche Center*

This accident is a tragic reminder that snow conditions can change dramatically from one day to the next and that even a relatively small avalanche can have devastating consequences in steep and rocky terrain. *(Source: Eastern Sierra Avalanche Center.)*

SKIER-TRIGGERED AVALANCHE
Washington, North Cascades, Slate Mountain

On Wednesday, March 15, a skier and a snowboarder departed from Heather Meadows near the Mt. Baker Ski Area, planning to climb and descend both Herman and Slate mountains. They climbed the south side of Mt. Herman to 6,000 feet (about 250 feet below the top) and then descended an eastern aspect. During the descent, the snowboarder triggered a shallow slab avalanche atop a short, steep rollover just above the traverse to Slate Mountain.

The pair then climbed the east side of Slate to its 6,209-foot summit. At around 1 p.m., they began their descent by a series of connected chute and ramp features on the southeast face, a line known locally as the Dog Leg or Z Couloir. The skier descended first and triggered a size D2.5 slab avalanche at the very top of the run. He was caught and quickly carried out of sight. The avalanche pushed him through very steep, rugged terrain and over a 200-to-250-foot terraced cliff. He came to rest on a low-angle slope below the face.

The snowboarder called for the skier on a radio and searched the path visually and with his avalanche transceiver. He found his partner on the snow surface, verbally responsive but not alert to person, place, time, or events. The skier had sustained significant injuries, including a deep head wound with an associated concussion, an open femur fracture, and a pelvis fracture.

The snowboarder used his phone to initiate rescue efforts within 10 to 12 minutes of the avalanche. He assessed and stabilized the skier as well as possible, given the location, available resources, and extent of injuries. A rescue helicopter from Naval Air Station Whidbey Island arrived at about 3:30 p.m., and both the skier and snowboarder were evacuated. The skier spent extensive time in the hospital for treatment of his injuries, which led to an amputation above the knee on the injured leg.

The southeast face of Slate Mountain consists of rocky, sparsely treed terrain broken by numerous cliffs. All lines of descent require extensive travel on 35°–45° terrain, in addition to navigation around rock buttresses and large cliffs.

The month prior to the avalanche was marked by extended periods of snowfall at cold temperatures, alternating with high pressure. March 6 to 9 brought sun, near-freezing mid-day temperatures, and light winds. This combination allowed for surface warming on southerly aspects. Rollerballs and other signs of warming were observed during this period.

From March 10 to 14, a series of storms produced two to three feet of new snow at a similar elevation and aspect to the avalanche site. Gradually clearing skies and mild temperatures on March 14 were followed by a few inches of new snow in the early morning of March 15, transitioning to partly cloudy skies and mild temperatures by midmorning.

A sun crust had formed during the high pressure from March 6 to 9, and the new snow formed a slab on top of it. The avalanche bed surface is believed to have been the crust buried on March 10. The avalanche began on a slope estimated at 40° and left a crown estimated at 1.5 to 2 feet high, approximately 50 feet wide at the start zone. *(Source: Northwest Avalanche Center.)*

*Editor's Note: The avalanche hazard was rated "moderate" for the day of the slide (the second highest of five levels). The first lines of the forecast read, "You can still trigger slab avalanches in steep terrain. Stick to moderately angled slopes and navigate around trigger points like convex rolls, unsupported terrain above or around cliffs, or wind loaded slopes just below ridgeline."

FALL IN COULOIR | Unplanned Descent Line, Ski Released
Colorado, Sangre de Cristo Mountains, Little Bear Peak

On April 15, I (male, 33) took a 350-foot fall while skiing down a north-facing couloir that falls from the west ridge of Little Bear Peak (14,041 feet). I had been hoping to complete an early spring solo of the Little Bear to Blanca traverse, followed by a ski descent off Blanca Peak (14,350 feet).

I started the approach the previous afternoon, shooting for a weather window between 10 p.m. and 3 a.m. for the traverse, with a planned bivy near Blanca Peak. The weather was great at the start, but conditions began to deteriorate as I reached Lake Como, directly below the couloir, around 7 p.m. I decided to keep pushing and ascend the couloir (part of the standard route up Little Bear), but the snow was very soft and deep, so the ascent took two hours. As I reached the top of the couloir, the wind and snow made visibility by headlamp impossible, so I stopped to bivy against a rock face below the ridgeline. In the morning, the wind was still whipping pretty badly, so I decided to forgo the summit and traverse attempt.

I packed up camp, put on my skis, and began my descent. The snow was good (powder with a slight crust in places). Everything seemed fine until my fourth turn, when my outside ski released and shot down the mountain. I had a Whippet pole and tried to self-arrest, but could not find solid purchase with the Whippet. I ended up on my back and began sliding into a chute with rocks on either side. My body rotated and I hit one shoulder and the side of my head on the rocks,

A skier captured images of his own sliding fall down a couloir on Little Bear Peak, a Colorado 14er. He impacted rocks in the choke but fortunately stopped soon below and was not very seriously injured. *Dan Apodaca*

then began to tomahawk down the slope as my second ski caught on the rocks and ejected. I landed feet-first in some deep powder, felt a sharp pain in my knee, then went face-first into the snow. Luckily, I was still holding my Whippet, and I was able to self-arrest before falling the rest of the way down the couloir.

I had some minor bruising on my shoulder and a tweaked knee, and my head felt a little foggy. I had been wearing a Petzl climbing helmet, and it sustained most of the damage. I stabilized my knee with a metal piece of my pack and an ACE bandage, and was able to self-rescue back to the car.

ANALYSIS

Every time I venture into the mountains, I keep safety in the forefront of my mind. I checked avalanche conditions (the hazard was "low" at all elevations), watched the weather, wore a helmet, and was acutely aware of my surroundings and skill level going into this adventure. The snow conditions in the couloir were variable, but I felt very comfortable with the idea of skiing down.

There was no damage to the bottom of my skis indicating I had hit a rock, nor any issues with my boots. (I was using G3 ZED 12 bindings and Scarpa Maestrale RS boots.) What I would have done differently is to triple-check that there was nothing obstructing the binding's pins in my boots, and I would have chosen to lock the toe bindings. Locking the toes creates its own risks, but it would lower the probability an unexpected release in no-fall terrain.

I did not plan to descend that couloir and was not intending to ski terrain with such high consequences. When attempting a decent like this, it would have been prudent to have a partner in the event of an accident. *(Source: Dan Apodaca.)*

DATA TABLES

These tables include data from all accidents in the United States and Canada that are reported in this book, plus additional accidents for which data were available. Many climbing accidents each year are not reported. [*For 2022, fewer reports than usual were received from Kentucky, West Virginia, and certain other areas.*] Therefore, these tables should not be viewed as precise counts of annual climbing accidents, and the data may not represent trends completely accurately. Readers likely will find the most value in the distribution and patterns of accident demographics and causes in Tables II and III.

TABLE I: REPORTED CLIMBING ACCIDENTS*

Year	Accidents Reported		Injured		Fatalities	
	US	CAN	US	CAN	US	CAN
1950s	33	n/a	26	n/a	10	n/a
1960s	66	8	52	7	21	3
1970s	114	18	97	10	34	8
1980s	191	29	124	26	33	8
1990	136	25	125	24	24	4
1991	169	20	147	11	18	6
1992	175	17	144	11	43	6
1993	132	27	121	17	21	1
1994	158	25	131	25	27	5
1995	168	24	134	18	37	7
1996	139	28	100	16	31	6
1997	158	35	148	24	31	13
1998	138	24	138	18	20	1
1999	123	29	91	20	17	10
2000	150	23	121	23	24	7
2001	150	22	138	14	16	2
2002	139	27	105	23	34	6
2003	118	29	105	22	18	6
2004	160	35	140	16	35	14
2005	111	19	85	14	34	7
2006	109	n/a	89	n/a	21	n/a
2007	113	n/a	95	n/a	15	n/a
2008	112	n/a	96	n/a	19	n/a
2009	126	n/a	112	n/a	23	n/a
2010	185	n/a	151	n/a	34	n/a
2011	157	n/a	109	n/a	29	n/a
2012	140	15	121	12	30	2
2013	143	11	100	5	21	4
2014	112	10	89	8	28	1
2015	173	20	111	16	37	4
2016	175	23	134	17	32	6

Year	Accidents Reported		Injured		Fatalities	
	US	CAN	US	CAN	US	CAN
2017	162	24	116	19	34	2
2018	187	17	198	12	17	5
2019	202	18	148	12	31	9
2020	157	19	118	13	28	5
2021	149	11	133	8	28	4
2022	170	22	96	14	40	6
2023	184	31	147	37	51	7
TOTAL	**8,867**	**1,179**	**7,321**	**888**	**1,891**	**347**

* Table I was revised in 2021. The figures presented for the 1950s, 1960s, 1970s, and 1980s are averages of the annual totals for each decade. The category "Total Persons Involved" has been eliminated. The "Total" figures are comprehensive totals from 1951 through 2022. The complete Table I from 1951 to 2019 is archived at publications.americanalpineclub.org.

TABLE II: REPORTED ACCIDENTS BY LOCATION*

Canada*	1959–2022		2023		
Geographic Districts	Accidents	Deaths	Accidents	Deaths	Injured
Alberta	628	169	12	2	19
British Columbia	375	140	10	5	10
Yukon & Northwest Territories	48	32	1	0	0
Ontario	43	9	2	0	2
Québec	42	10	6	0	6
Eastern Provinces & Territories	9	2	0	0	0

United States*	1951–2022		2023		
Geographic Districts	Accidents	Deaths	Accidents	Deaths	Injured
Alaska	701	237	20	3	26
Arizona, Nevada, Texas	155	28	12	1	10
Northeast	1339	173	23	1	22
Southeast	324	47	11	2	9
California	1756	367	42	11	32
Central	154	20	3	1	1
Colorado	1162	289	16	6	12
Montana, Idaho, South Dakota	129	50	7	2	7
Oregon	331	142	7	4	5
Utah, New Mex.	303	84	12	4	9
Washington	2118	367	16	11	4
Wyoming	713	172	15	5	10

* The Canada section of Table II was revised in 2021. Eastern Provinces and Territories includes Nunavut, Newfoundland, and the Maritimes. In the U.S., Northeast includes New England and the Mid-Atlantic states (southward to Maryland/Delaware), plus Ohio and Indiana. Southeast includes West Virginia, Virginia, Kentucky, and states farther south. Central incudes Michigan and the Upper Midwest (minus South Dakota), plus Missouri and Arkansas.

TABLE III: ACCIDENT CHARACTERISTICS AND CAUSES

	1951–2022 USA	1959–2022 CAN*	2023 USA	2023 CAN
Terrain				
Rock	6107	642	122	19
Snow	2913	393	45	5
Ice	344	34	10	6
Water	27	3	1	0
Unknown	40	12	0	0
Ascent or Descent				
Ascent	4837	699	91	18
Descent	1732	434	58	6
Unknown[1]	425	20	29	4
Other[1]	91	9	8	3
Climbing Style[†]				
Alpine/Mountaineering	202	20	66	10
Ice and mixed climbing	16	5	11	6
Traditional rock climbing	167	11	50	10
Sport climbing	100	11	22	2
Big-wall climbing	4	0	3	0
Bouldering	19	4	7	3
Top-rope	13	0	1	0
Free solo or DWS	20	3	4	0
Ski mountaineering	29	5	8	3
Other/Not Applicable/Unknown	32	1	21	5
Rope Position[†]				
Leading	202	24	39	9
Seconding	10	0	3	0
Top-roping	8	0	4	0
Roped but not belayed	8	2	4	0
Unroped	165	17	59	8
Rappelling	67	5	13	7
Lowering	23	0	8	0
Belaying	18	3	4	3
Other/Not Applicable/Unknown	121	15	85	15

[†] "Climbing Style" and "Rope Position" categories were introduced in 2021. (The first two columns for each category include data from 2019–2022.) "Rope Position" tabulates the position or activity of the person(s) most directly affected by an accident (injured or killed, stranded, near miss, etc.), at the time the incident occurred. "Roped but not belayed" includes simul-climbing and glacier travel. "Unroped" includes bouldering.

	1951–2022 USA	1959–2022 CAN*	2023 USA	2023 CAN
Immediate Causes**				
Fall on rock	4560	362	63	12
Fall on ice (formerly snow or ice)	1280	228	5	2
Fall on snow	41	1	15	0
Falling rock, ice, object	767	160	15	4
Illness	484	28	14	0
Stranded / Lost	510	73	6	8
Avalanche	361	146	8	4
Rappel Failure/Error[3]	485	65	13	1
Lowering Error[6]	55	3	7	0
Fall from anchor	4	0	4	1
Anchor failure	13	1	2	0
Exposure	297	14	6	1
Glissade error	251	18	0	0
Protection pulled out	394	0	1	0
Failure to follow route	262	36	0	0
Fall into crevasse/moat	204	53	1	1
Faulty use of crampons	128	7	0	0
Ascending too fast	93	0	0	0
Skiing[4]	98	20	1	0
Lightning	69	7	0	0
Equipment failure	19	3	0	0
Other[5]	666	45	10	0
Unknown	127	15	19	1
Contributing Causes***				
Climbing unroped	1178	181	20	1
Inexperience	1151	211	7	9
Placed no/inadequate protection	966	117	6	0
Inadequate equipment/clothing	801	79	5	0
Weather	572	84	0	0
Climbing alone	492	75	0	0
No helmet	421	77	0	0
Inadequate belay	339	31	0	0
Protection pulled out (climber placed)	46	4	9	4
Protection pulled out (fixed)	4	0	1	0
Inadequate knot	6	0	2	0
Inadequate backup	17	0	3	0
Rope too short	4	1	4	0
Poor position	293	39	8	0

	1951–2022 USA	1959–2022 CAN*	2023 USA	2023 CAN
Darkness	199	24	0	0
Party separated	148	14	1	0
Loose rock/failure to test holds	187	59	18	4
Off-route	161	23	0	1
Failure to self-arrest	14	0	5	0
Exposure	79	16	7	1
Illness	61	10	2	0
Equipment failure	31	8	1	0
Other	419	116	40	9
Age of Individuals				
Under 15	1258	12	1	0
15-20	1393	208	4	1
21-25	1775	264	27	1
26-30	1681	232	20	6
31-35	2297	23	21	0
36-50	3699	152	19	3
Over 50	550	41	23	0
Unknown	2684	667	81	30
Sex[6]				
Male	1019	105	115	15
Female	296	26	37	5
Not known	217	46	48	25
Experience Level				
Novice	2041	311	16	1
Intermediate	1979	371	18	2
Expert	2922	551	79	19
Unknown	3156	656	84	13
Month				
January	302	29	6	1
February	292	64	10	3
March	457	85	4	2
April	554	51	13	3
May	1163	77	29	4
June	1450	96	23	2
July	2247	286	24	4
August	1327	225	15	4
September	2155	90	13	4
October	606	48	12	0
November	308	25	12	1

	1951–2022 USA	1959–2022 CAN*	2023 USA	2023 CAN
December	163	29	4	2
Unknown	117	3	3	1

Type of Injury/Illness (Data since 1984. Fracture and internal injury breakouts introduced in 2021.)

	1951–2022 USA	1959–2022 CAN*	2023 USA	2023 CAN
Fracture: lower extremity	111	11	30	6
Fracture: upper extremity	20	4	1	0
Fracture: other	42	2	3	0
Spine injury/fracture	42	3	4	0
Total Fractures	2080	285	38	6
Laceration	939	93	9	3
Abrasion	495	81	4	0
Bruise	665	92	4	0
Sprain/Strain	537	41	13	5
Head Injury/TBI	481	45	10	2
Internal: chest	11	0	0	0
Internal: abdomen	4	0	1	0
Hypothermia	208	20	4	0
Frostbite	175	13	7	1
Dislocation	195	17	4	0
Puncture	71	14	1	0
Acute mountain sickness	57	0	0	0
HAPE	110	1	4	0
HACE	44	1	2	0
Other[7]	564	72	10	0
None	496	215	14	18

[*] No Canada data from 2006–2011; includes new data from 2012–2023

[**] "Fall on snow" and "anchor failure" were added in 2021, starting with 2019 data. (Past editions combined falls on snow and ice.) "Protection pulled out" combines two former categories; in this section, the protection pulling out must directly cause the fall. Data from 2022 incidents is missing.

[***] Categories introduced in 2021, starting with 2019 data, include "Protection pulled out (climber placed)" and "Protection pulled out (fixed)"; these replaced "Nut/cam pulled out" and "Piton/ice screw pulled out." Other new categories in 2021 were "Inadequate knot," "Inadequate backup," "Rope too short," and "Failure to self-arrest." Data from 2022 incidents is missing.

[1] Some reported accidents happen when climbers are at the top or bottom of a route, during an approach, or in camp. This category was created in 2001. The category "unknown" primarily reflects solo climbers.

[2] These are illnesses/injuries that led directly or indirectly to an accident or rescue, such as HAPE.

[3] Prior years included some lowering errors, anchor failures, and inadequate backups (now their own categories).

[4] This category covers ski mountaineering. Backcountry ski touring or snowshoeing incidents, including those involving avalanches, are not counted in these tables.

[5] These included broken ice dam, impaled on cam lobe, and rope severed by carabiner.

[6] Categories introduced in 2016.

[7] These included snakebite, crushed by boulder, compartment syndrome, and others. Note: Injuries are counted only once in each category for a given incident. For example, an accident that results in two broken ankles will be listed once under "Fracture: lower extremity."

CLIMBERS HELPING CLIMBERS SINCE 1959.

Alison Sheets.

MOUNTAIN **RESCUE** ASSOCIATION

We Never Charge for Rescue

Courage. Commitment. Compassion.

www.mra.org